NOT CHOSEN
TO
SALVATION

An Answer to David Nettleton's Book
"Chosen To Salvation"

A VERSE-BY-VERSE EXAMINATION OF
SCRIPTURE THAT EXPOSES THE FALSE DOCTRINE
OF PREDESTINATION AND ILLUMINATES THE
FREE WILL AND RESPONSIBILITY OF MAN.

*"For God so loved the world, that he gave his only
begotten Son, that whosoever believeth in him should not
perish, but have everlasting life." – John 3:16*

By Dr. Max D. Younce

NOT CHOSEN TO SALVATION

An Answer to David Nettleton's Book,
"Chosen to Salvation"

By Dr. Max D. Younce,
P.O. Box 573
Walnut Grove, MN 56180
Web: www.heritagebbc.com

Unless otherwise indicated, all Scripture quotations are
taken from the King James Translation of the Bible.

Library of Congress Control Number: 2008910085
ISBN Number: 978-0-9815225-4-8
Second Printing

"False Doctrine Shipwrecks Souls"

Printed In the USA By
Morris Publishing®
3212 E. Hwy. 30
Kearney, NE 68847

ACKNOWLEDGEMENTS

Our first printing was in book form on 8-1/2 x 11 paper. Hundreds have gone out to missionaries, pastors, Bible colleges, etc., throughout the U.S. and abroad. This could not have been accomplished without the help of Mr. Bill McKay and Mr. and Mrs. Cassell, members of our church.

Mr. Bill McKay, owner of C.S.Q.P. Printing in N. Olmstead, Ohio, did the original printing. Bill is a personal friend who gave me great assistance in design, typesetting, and financial help, without which the book could not have been printed at that time.

Harold and Patricia Cassell, who spent untold numbers of hours in collating and binding thousands of copies. Their enthusiasm and cheerful attitude has been more than encouraging.

TABLE OF CONTENTS

vi

THE LIGHTHOUSE OF GOD'S WORD

God's Word is a lighthouse revealing rocks of sin,
Illuminating false doctrine before it enters in.

"God so loved the world," that's each and every man
"Not willing... any should perish" was the purpose of His Plan.

Ordained before the world began and accomplished by our Lord.
"Whosoever will may come" is the message of God's Word.

If you live in shadows where the lighthouse does not glow,
False doctrine may wreck your vessel before His truth you know.

"Predestinated to be conformed to the image of his son,"
At the Rapture this will happen, First John Three, Verse One.

God did not choose some for Heaven and others to go to Hell,
That's what they mean by "T-U-L-I-P," they just don't want to tell.

They do despite to the Grace of God, and Christ's death sacrificially,.
"And I, if I be lifted up from the earth, will draw all men unto me."

Read Isaiah, Chapter 53, Verse Six. Read it very carefully.
"Go in at the first all...out at the last all, you'll be saved eternally."

Thank God for the "whosoevers" and the "alls" revealed in His Word.
You have no excuse to reject the truth because you now have heard.

God never gives you the faith with which to believe.
He gives you the truth in His Word which you must receive.

Believe Christ died for you as full payment for your sin,
And when the time comes to go to Heaven, you will enter in.

" Believe on the Lord Jesus Christ, and thou shalt be saved,..." Acts 16:31

"False Doctrine Shipwrecks Souls"

PREFACE

This book was not written to present evidence for winning a popularity contest. Allow me to qualify this statement. Many times a writer will seek to support his views concerning a subject or doctrine by quoting other men who share his same ideas. One book in particular devoted approximately 90 pages in quoting Articles of the G.A.R.B.C., confessions of faith, theologians, Bible teachers and preachers. I would have to say that the author had gone to great lengths to align my thinking with his. The only problem is, I would be persuaded by a group of names instead of God's Word. I think the middle verse of the Bible should be considered,

"It is better to trust in the Lord than to put confidence in man" - Psalm 118:8

I have purposely eliminated quotes, statements and sermons from men of renown from the text, as I desire the reader to draw his own conclusions from the Word of God, not the word of men. Also, I could have listed and quoted a multiplicity of Bible colleges, theologians, pastors, Bible teachers and, literally, thousands of Christians who believe just as I. But this is not my purpose. The Bible will speak for Itself.

"To the law and to the testimony: if they speak not according to this word, it is because there is no light in them" - Isaiah 8:20

In our examination of the passages of Scripture that deal with predestination, choosing and election, I have endeavored to view these verses in their context and correlate other verses that speak on the same subject. In so doing, one will always have the true mind of God as one Scripture cannot contradict another without giving birth to a false doctrine.

With a thorough knowledge of God's Word on a certain subject, a Christian then possesses a solid foundation which will stand firm against the showers of false teaching.

I pray this book will be a blessing and encouragement to you as we walk together through the Bible, viewing God's Word on this great subject.

"False Doctrine Shipwrecks Souls"

IN APPRECIATION

This book is in dedication to my wonderful wife, Marge. Her patience and encouragement is unsurpassed during the many night hours spent in writing this book, not to mention the hours she spent in typing, retyping and making corrections in the manuscripts (Proverbs 31:10).

May I also extend my deepest appreciation to the members of Heritage Bible Church for their love, patience, and support in seeing this book completed. They are a tremendous group of Christian people whom I have the privilege to pastor.

I am also deeply indebted to two great men of God. Dr. Thomas Duff (now deceased), pastor of the Troy Baptist Temple in Troy, Ohio, who led me to Christ. It was here I was first taught the great truths and doctrines of the Word of God. The second is Dr. Mark G. Cambron, a past president and founder of Seaside Mission and president of Florida Bible College. He was one of the great Bible teachers, and is now with the Lord. It was my privilege to study under Dr. Cambron where these giant Bible truths and doctrines were amplified. - 2 Timothy 2:2.

- Dr. Max D. Younce

PURPOSE OF THE BOOK

The purpose of this book is four-fold; to show that God is justified in judging the lost, to illuminate the false doctrine of election and pre-destination concerning salvation and service, to reveal that man is totally responsible for his actions and decisions, to repudiate the mutilation and distortion of God's Word in Dr. Nettleton's book, "Chosen to Salvation."

1.   God is justified.

If God elected some for Heaven and not others, He cannot be justified as a righteous God since we have...

> *"....all have sinned and come short of the glory of God."*

Rather, the Word of God states:

> *"For God so loved the WORLD, that he gave his only begotten Son, that WHOSOEVER believeth in him should not perish, but have everlasting life." - John 3:16*

Since God loved the world, paid for the sins of the world, and gives anyone in the world (whosoever) the opportunity to be saved, then God is justified while the false doctrine of election to salvation is found unjustifiable.

2. False doctrine illuminated.

False doctrine can only be built upon bits and pieces of Scripture, extracted out of context and clothed with humanistic ideologies. Restoring these Scriptures and examining them in their proper context will restore a solid foundation of sound doctrine and illuminate the false doctrine of predestination and election for salvation. We are told in 2 Timothy 2:15 to *"rightly divide the word of truth."* We are not to whack out pieces of Scripture to support our own man-made doctrine!

3. Man is totally responsible.

If election to salvation is true, then man has no freewill of his own; therefore, he must do as he is programmed to do. No, we are not robots but thinking beings, created of God. God gave Adam and Eve the freewill to obey or disobey when He placed them in Eden. The right of choice and freewill has been extended to every individual since then. Therefore, man is totally responsible for his own destiny since God....

> *"...is longsuffering to us-ward, not willing that any should perish, but that all should come to repentance"* - 2 Peter 3:9.

4. Chosen to Salvation by Nettleton (pub. by Regular Baptist Press).

I was advised they would consider my book for publication if I did not attack Mr. Nettleton on his book. This I rejected as I do not want to be restricted in my writing, especially concerning a major doctrine. I do not want to forfeit my liberty in referring to a book or its author that I am convinced is in error with the Scriptures. Mr. Nettleton has been on the Council of 18 several times and surely does not represent the entire populace of the G.A.R.B.C. with his book. I invite any interested to examine with me the misuse of

Scripture and the false doctrine it supports of God electing some to salvation.

As you read this book, you may feel that I have been unkind in some of my statements. I only feel we should be as forthright in refuting false doctrine as those who are projecting it. If you have studied the life of Christ in the New Testament you will recall that Christ rebuked the false teachers, labeling them as hypocrites - Matthew 23. He called those who lied liars - John 8:39-47. He called those who committed immoral acts adulterers - Luke 16:18. A false doctrine is a Satanic doctrine--of demons--and this needs to be realized -1 Timothy 4:1-2,

> *"Now the Spirit speaketh expressly, that in the latter times some shall depart from the faith, giving heed to seducing spirits, and doctrines of devils; (1) Speaking lies in hypocrisy; having their conscience seared with a hot iron;"* (2)

The "doctrine of election to salvation" is not some mini-doctrine that one can have the attitude towards, "Well, it doesn't amount to that much. Let's not make an issue over it." This is exactly what Satan would like. No, it is not a minor doctrine, it is one of the major doctrines of the Bible. When you project a doctrine that attacks the character of God (making Him unjust) and the Word of God (making It contradict Itself), you have a Satanic false doctrine.

The roots of this doctrine produce many branches of corrupt theology which are not clearly seen on the surface, nor admitted to by their proponents. In order to stimulate our thinking and hone our minds prior to reading this book, may I submit one such case in point? I will quote a section from David Nettleton's book, *Chosen to Salvation*, page 22, in its entirety for analysis:

> "Election to service. 'Ye have not chosen me, but
> I have chosen you, and ordained you, that ye should

go and bring forth fruit, and that your fruit should remain...' (John 15:15). God does ordain some to service. In the case of Jeremiah He said, 'Before I formed thee in the belly I knew thee; and before thou camest forth out of the womb I sanctified thee, and I ordained thee a prophet unto the nations' (Jeremiah 1:5). Likewise it was said of John the Baptist before he was conceived that 'he shall be filled with the Holy Ghost, even from his mother's womb' (Luke 1:15). This filling was for service. 'And many of the children of Israel shall he turn to the Lord their God (Luke 1:16).

Since God chooses some individuals to serve Him, surely He chooses to save them first, since His saved ones serve Him.

The entire plan is God's--the salvation, the means of salvation and the service which is the result."

In analyzing the last paragraph we find a lot of confusion in Nettleton's conclusion. Read it carefully and notice what he says, "His saved ones serve Him." Allow me to ask you, is this true according to the Word of God? Of course not! Was Peter lost when he denied Christ three times? (Matthew 26:69-75). Was Lot lost when we hardly find anything complimentary in Scripture concerning his life? 2 Peter 2:7,8 tells us he was saved.

The book of 1 Corinthians was written to one of the most carnal churches that ever existed, yet they were saved as we find in 1 Corinthians 1:2. Nettleton leads his readers to believe you are not really saved if you are not serving the Lord. This is very confusing to a new Christian and in sharp contrast to God's Word.

For example, in John 1:12 we become a child of God or a son of God by receiving Christ. In Hebrews 12:5-8 God tells the Christians that He will chasten or correct His children for sin because He loves them. In Verses 5-8 He reminds us five times that we are still His sons and not lost, even when disobedient. In 1st Corinthians 3:14 we are assured of rewards for serving Christ. In Verse 15 we are told that we can lose our rewards for lack of service, but we are still saved. If one continues Nettleton's statement to its conclusion, you end up with nothing but confusion.

1. All the saved will serve. Not true. This is the "front door" approach to false doctrine.

2. If you are not serving, you are not saved. *Not true.* This is the "back door" approach to false doctrine.

3. If Number 2 is true, then salvation is by works. *Not true* --Ephesians 2:8,9.

4. If Number 1 is true, then very subtly the doctrine of eradication of the sin nature springs forth. *Not true.* (Read Romans 7:14-25). The Christian has a battle with the old nature until the Rapture, when he receives his new body.

5. In reference to Number 1, then everyone who appears to be serving Christ is saved. *Not true*, for you cannot tell if a person is saved by the way they live. Matthew 7:22-23 exposes the counterfeit Christian possessing wonderful works, but not believing the right message. The only way you can tell if a person is a Christian is if they are trusting Christ as Savior, plus nothing. That Christian may or may not possess good works!

6. An example of another stem of false doctrine growing from these roots is revealed. Let's say that you are serving Christ, but get discouraged and stop. Were you saved to begin with? Did you lose your salvation? Did God become unfaithful to His Word and promise of eternal life because we became unfaithful to Him? *Not true.* God's faithfulness to His Word *never* depends on our faithfulness! Remember, these are stems that continue to grow from the roots of "Chosen to Salvation."

7. *Complete confusion* is the result of the statement, "His saved ones serve Him." Let us analyze this. If I am saved, I will serve. If I am not serving, I am not saved; therefore, I am elected to serve with no will to do otherwise.

If I do not have a will to disobey or sin, then I would have to have had my old sinful nature eradicated. If I have no sin nature since I am saved, how can I lose my rewards at the Judgment Seat of Christ as I would never have ceased to serve Christ?

I hope you can begin to see the confusion that is caused and the undercurrents that roar in opposition to God's Word. On the surface "His saved ones serve Him" seems very smooth, but a deeper examination of the undercurrents only shows God's Word in agitation crying, "No, No, that is not true!"

"False Doctrine Shipwrecks Souls"

"There are so many theories today concerning foreknowledge, predestination and election, until the mind of the normal and average Christian is so mixed up that he doesn't know what to believe. If we do not get these three doctrines straight, our whole Christian life will be warped, and soul winning will become a lost grace."

- Dr. Mark G. Cambron

"In whom the god of this world hath blinded the minds of them which believe not, lest the light of the glorious gospel of Christ, who is the image of God, should shine unto them." - 2 Corinthians 4:4

"False Doctrine Shipwrecks Souls"

CHAPTER ONE

EXPLAINING PREDESTINATION AND FOREKNOWLEDGE

The word "predestination" comes from the Greek verb "proorizo." It means, according to *Vine's Expository Words on the Greek New Testament*, to "mark out beforehand, to determine before, foreordain." In essence, "predestination" means that something has been predicted by God and it must and will come to pass.

The word "predestinate" as translated in the KJV is found only twice; that being in Romans 8:29 and 30. "Predestinated" is found only twice and that is in Ephesians; once in Ephesians 1:5 and once in 1:11. These two words do not appear in the Old Testament.

We shall examine who is predestinated, what event is predestinated and when it will take place.

A. Ephesians 1:5 - Redemption Of The Body At The Rapture

Let us begin with Ephesians 1:5...

> *"Having predestinated us unto the adoption of children by Jesus Christ to Himself, according to the good pleasure of his will."*

Notice who is predestinated. It can only be one of two groups: the saved or the lost. Paul identifies the children of God as the object of being predestinated, *"Having predestinated us* (plural pronoun)." This is Paul and every saved person. God did not predestinate anyone to be saved, but this teaches He predestinated something for those who are already saved.

What did God predestinate for the Christian? The Scriptures are pure and simple. The Christian is predestinated <u>unto</u> the adoption of children (Greek, HUIOTHESIA, meaning sonship). When we trust Christ as our Savior, we become His children:

> *"But as many as received him, to them gave he power to become the sons (Greek, TEKNON, meaning-a child.) of God, even to them that believeth on his name." - John 1:12*

We are positioned in Heaven as a <u>son</u> now, but we do not come to the realization of our sonship until the Rapture.

The Jewish Bar Mitzvah may aid in understanding adoption and sonship. Bar Mitzvah means "a son of the commandments, or the placing of a son." When a Jewish boy reaches the age of 13, he is then considered as a adult. He is expected to accept adult religious responsibilities. It is a joyful occasion accompanied by gifts from friends and family. He is no longer considered a <u>child</u>, but an adult <u>son</u>.

The word "adoption" is derived from the Greek word "huiothesia," from "huios", meaning "a son" and "thesis" "a placing." Therefore, "the placing of a son." Just as a Jewish boy is placed as an adult son on the day he reaches 13, we Christians also experience our sonship when we are placed in Heaven at the day of the Rapture. This is when we have our physical bodies redeemed for a new glorified body. It could be no clearer than stated in Romans 8:23:

> *"And not only they, but ourselves also, which have the first fruits of the spirit, even we ourselves groan within ourselves, WAITING FOR THE ADOPTION, TO WIT, THE REDEMPTION OF OUR BODY."*

In summary:

WHO: Negative: Nowhere are the lost said to be predestinated to be saved.

Positive: The saved are predestinated to receive something.

WHAT: The Adoption. Romans 8:23, "the adoption, to wit, the redemption of our body."

WHEN: At the Rapture. 1 Thessalonians 4:17, 1 Corinthians 15:50-54.

B. Ephesians 1:11,12.- This Is Not Our Testimony

> *"In whom also we have obtained an inheritance, being predestinated according to the purpose of him who worketh all things after the counsel of his own will: that we should be to the praise of his glory, who first trusted in Christ."*

Notice the use of the word *"we"*, a plural pronoun. Paul is including himself and all Christians. They have obtained an inheritance. This identifies those who are predestinated for something as being <u>already</u> saved. We can see in Verse 12 what the Christian is predestinated to receive.

What is predestinated is according to the Lord's purpose. He will also bring it to pass *"after the counsel <u>of his own will</u>."* *"His own will"* lets us know that God does not leave what He predestinated to be brought to pass by the volition or faithfulness of man. Therefore, we can rest assured... what God predestinated <u>will</u> come to pass!

In summary: The saved are the recipients of being predestinated. It was God's purpose to do so and He will bring it to pass Himself. We are told in Verse 12 <u>what</u> is predestinated:

> *"That we (Christians) should be to the praise of his glory, who first trusted in Christ."*

At first glance one may think this means it is God's will that every Christian should lead a separated life, which would be to the praise of His glory. This is certainly God's will for every believer (Romans 12:1,2). However, this cannot be the meaning of this verse, if taken in context, as the fulfillment of what was predestinated. If this were true, then it has not come to pass in every Christian's life. Remember, what God predestinates <u>will</u>, without exception, come to pass. The reason being, every Christian is the recipient of what is predestinated. Not every Christian leads a separated life. In fact, some Christians never lead a separated life from the time they are saved until they leave this earth!

To what is this referring? It has reference to the event of the Rapture when, without exception, every Christian will be to the praise of His glory. The Bridegroom (Christ) is looking in expectation for His Bride (the Church). The Church (every believer) is looking for the Bridegroom to return and so shall we ever be with the Lord. This meeting is the fulfillment of what Christ predestinated for every believer. Remember-- what is predestinated <u>must come to pass</u>.

24

If *"to the praise of his glory"* meant leading a separated life, it may not come to pass, for all Christians are not yielding their lives to God's will. Christ never leaves what He predestinates to be fulfilled by the volition of man. By the determined will and power of God, the Rapture will fulfill every qualifying aspect of His predestination,

"that we should be to the praise of His glory."

C. Romans 8:29 - The Elements of "Foreknowledge" & "Predestination"

"For whom he did foreknow, he also did predestinate to be conformed to the image of his Son, that he might be the firstborn among many brethren."

The statement is heard many times, "You cannot reconcile the sovereignty of God and the free will of man." This is not true--one can understand both. The confusion exists when one does not properly understand the meaning of foreknowledge and predestination. Foreknowledge is an attribute of God's omniscience. Primarily, foreknowledge had to do with persons and places, and predestination is centered in God's purposes.

Foreknowledge contains ONE element, that is, knowing what is going to happen before it takes place. In relation to people and places, it does not contain the element of bringing it to pass or making it happen.

Predestination, on the other hand, is different from foreknowledge in that it contains TWO elements: One is the prediction (His omniscience) and the other is the act of God (His omnipotence) to bring it to pass. The confusion begins when one inserts meanings into a word which it does not contain. Remember, keep these two words separated as to their meaning.

Foreknowledge has ONE element, that of foreknowing what is going to happen. Do not add any other meanings to this word, it contains one element only!

Predestination has TWO elements; one is predicting, the other fulfilling. Again, predestination is related to God's purposes, foreknowledge is related to persons and places.

In Verse 29 we are told:

"For whom he (Christ) did foreknow..."

This simply states that Christ knew ahead of time every person who would trust Him as their Savior. The word carries no other element which would impede the free will of a person to make their own choice. Every Christian who would be saved is foreknown of God. We also see that every Christian is going to be the recipient of what God is going to predestinate.

"For whom he did foreknow (every Christian) He also did <u>predestinate</u>."

He foreknew every person who would be saved. His purpose is seen in predestination as we are predestinated to what?

"To be conformed to the image of his son."

When will we be conformed to the image of God's Son? At the Rapture, of course!

In Philippians 3:20,21 we are told:

"For our conversation is in heaven; from whence also we look for the Saviour, the Lord Jesus Christ. Who shall change our vile body, that it may be fashioned like unto his glorious body."

This is being conformed to the image of His Son.

In 1st John 3:2 we read:

"Beloved, now are we the sons (Greek, TEKNON, children) of God, and it doth not yet appear what we shall

be; but we know that, when he shall appear (Rapture) , WE
SHALL BE LIKE HIM; for we shall see him as he is."

Predestination becomes very clear if we do two things: One, take exactly what the Scripture says and believe it. Two, know the difference between foreknowledge and predestination and add no other elements of meaning to them. Foreknowledge has one element while predestination has two.

In summary: Verse 29 teaches the following according to predestination:

WHO: Only the saved are predestinated, not the lost.

WHAT: Christians are predestinated at some future time
          to *"be conformed to the image of His Son."*

WHEN: At the Rapture. Philippians 3:20, 21, and 1 John
        3:2.

D. Romans 8:30 - Who Are The Called?

"Moreover whom He (Christ) did predestinate, them he
also called: and whom he called, them he also justified: and
whom he justified, them he also glorified."

Let us briefly examine each aspect of this verse as we observe the simplicity of God's Word.

"Moreover whom He did predestinate."

As we have found, those who are predestinated are only Christians, never the lost to <u>be</u> saved.

"...them he also called..."

How are Christians called? The Scripture tells us in Romans 10:17 that:

"So then faith cometh by hearing and hearing by the
word of God."

And we are told in John 6:44:

> *"No man can come to me, except the father which hath sent me draw him."*

This verse is comparable to that of Romans 8:30. The phrases *"them he also called"* and *"draw him"* lead us to ask, "How then does God draw or call the lost?" In John 12:32 we have the answer:

> *"And I, if I (Christ) be lifted up from the earth, will draw all men unto me."*

"All men" here does not mean "all men without exception," but "all men without distinction of race, creed, social standing, etc."

We are called or drawn by the Word of God which testifies of the resurrection and ascension of our Lord. So then, if *"faith cometh by hearing and hearing by the Word of God,"* Christ will draw men by the hearing of the Word. This is the preaching of the Gospel:

> *"Moreover, brethren, I declare unto you the gospel which I preached unto you...how that Christ died for our sins according to the Scriptures; And that he was buried, and that he arose again the third day according to the Scriptures." - 1 Corinthians 15:1,3,4*

Christ never calls us outside of His Word (Romans 10:17). The called are those who have established His Word by accepting Christ as their personal Savior.

> *"...them he also justified..."*

All are declared righteous upon receiving Christ by faith. As it says in Romans 5:1,

> *"Therefore, being justified (declared righteous) by faith, we have peace with God through our Lord Jesus Christ."*

And those who are justified the Scripture tells us..

"...them he also glorified."

Notice the use of past tense here. This is a positional truth. God looks upon Christians as though they were already in Heaven.

Notice the past tense of Ephesians 2:6.

"And hath raised us up together, and made us sit together in heavenly places in Christ Jesus:" - Ephesians 2:6

In summary: Romans 8:30 simply teaches that the ones who were the object of God's predestination were already saved. For *"whom he did predestinate,"* these are the *"called, justified, and glorified."*

No one is ever predestinated to be saved. You must, personally, realize you have sinned and come short of the glory of God (Romans 3:23). God sent Christ to pay for our sin (2 Corinthians 5:21) so we do not have to pay that debt ourselves in Hell. If one will only believe in (trust) Jesus Christ as his Savior, God will give him eternal life.

"These things have I written unto you that believe on the name of the Son of God; that ye may know that ye have eternal life, and that ye may believe on the name of the Son of God." - 1 John 5:13

It should be recognized that all of the Old Testament prophecies could be stated as being predestinated. Other words synonymous with "predestinate" would be "foretelling, prophecy, predicting and etc." For God to predict the future of people, places and nations, he would have to foreknow the future.

We are grateful to God for His precious Word. There are thousands of prophecies where synonymous words are used instead of "predestinate." I have limited our study only to the four places where the actual word appears in the Bible--due to its misuse. Expanding any further into prophecy would constitute a book, or books, on that great subject!

*For the commandment is a lamp; and the law is light;
and reproofs of instruction are the way of life: - Proverbs
6:23*

"False Doctrine Shipwrecks Souls"

CHAPTER TWO

EXAMINING VERSES USED TO SUPPORT ELECTION

We are going to examine some of the verses that are used to endorse the doctrine of election to salvation. It is amazing how some will pull verses out of context that clearly have to do with service and God's provision for His saints and attempt to apply these to salvation. It is unbelievable to what extremes men will go in an attempt to prove this doctrine. They extract a line or verse from the context and apply it to support their particular false teaching.

1. Luke 4:25-29 - A Widow & A King, Chosen To Sustain A Prophet & Show God's Power

"But I tell you of a truth, many widows were in Israel in the days of Elias, when the heaven was shut up three years

and six months, when great famine was throughout all the land. (25)

But unto none of them was Elias sent, save unto Sarepta, a city of Sidon, unto a woman that was a widow. (26)

And many lepers were in Israel in the time of Eliseus the prophet; and none of them was cleansed, saving Naaman the Syrian. (27)

And all they in the synagogue, when they heard these things, were filled with wrath. (28)

And rose up, and thrust him out of the city, and led him unto the brow of the hill whereon their city was built, that they might cast him down headlong." Luke 4:25-29

Christ made these statements while speaking in the synagogue as an illustration. Now Mr. Nettleton gives his statement concerning these verses on page 26 of his book, *Chosen to Salvation*:

"One out of many widows was chosen, and one out of many lepers was cleansed. The result of such teaching was anger. Special mercy was shown to the widow and to the leper."

We are going to examine the Old Testament account more thoroughly and see what the real *purpose* of God was in directing Elijah to the widow's house. The record of Elijah going to the widow's home is found in 1 Kings 17:9. When we begin with the 17th Chapter of 1 Kings, we find that there had been a famine in the land and that Elijah had been by the brook, Cherith, that is the brook before Jordan. We find out here that Elijah had been fed by the ravens, but when the brook dried up God then directed him to go to this woman's

32

house. We are going to find out the purpose for this as it is a far cry from electing this woman, and then using this as an illustration for salvation as Nettleton has done.

It is hard for me to believe that someone would do this, when in reality, the Scriptures teach that God had a purpose for sending Elijah to this widow woman. This purpose is found in 1 Kings 17:9:

> *"Arise, get thee to Zarephath, which belongeth to Zidon, and dwell there: behold, I have commanded a widow woman there* to sustain thee."

The reason for this sustenance was that the brook had dried up. You will notice that in Verse 7 of this same chapter:

> *"And it came to pass after a while, that the brook dried up, because there had been no rain in the land."*

Therefore, God had directed Elijah to go to this particular town where the widow woman lived. She was to *sustain* him, *feed* him and to *water* him, as this was the *purpose* of God. For one to apply this to salvation is unbelievable!

Let us continue to read the entire story as found in 1 Kings, Chapter 17. We find that after the widow had fed Elijah and given him water, he stayed for a time. Now we pick up the story in 1 Kings 17:17,

> *"And it came to pass after these things, that the son of the woman, the mistress of the house, fell sick; and his sickness was so sore, that there was no breath left in him. (17)*
>
> *And she said unto Elijah, what have I to do with thee, O thou man of God? Art thou come unto me to call my sin to remembrance, and to slay my son?" (18)*

Perhaps the woman thought her son had been slain because of some past sin that she had committed. We do not know for sure as this is all that is given. But we find out that

Elijah had prayed to God for life to be restored to her son. God had seen fit to honor Elijah's prayer as *God had a purpose* in restoring his life again. He, evidently, had been dead for just a short period of time. Now, the record is found in Verses 22 to 24:

> *"And the Lord heard the voice of Elijah; and the soul of the child came into him again, and he revived. (22).*
>
> *And Elijah took the child, and brought him down out of the chamber into the house, and delivered him unto his mother: and Elijah said, See, thy son liveth. (23).*
>
> *And the woman said to Elijah, now by this I know that thou art a man of God, and that the word of the Lord in thy mouth is truth." (24).*

There was a twofold reason for God's directing Elijah to this woman's house. The first reason, of course, being that God had spoken to this woman to care for Elijah. We find this in Verse 9 of the 17th chapter, in the last part of the verse:

> *"...behold, I have commanded a widow woman there to sustain thee."*

So we see the first purpose of sending Elijah to the widow woman was to have her *sustain Elijah*. Could the Lord have stated it any clearer?

Nettleton cites this case as evidence and leverage to support his contention that some are elected to salvation. It would have been nice of Nettleton to have informed his readers of GOD'S PURPOSE for using the widow woman in sustaining Elijah. She could have been the only available person in the vicinity that was saved, we do not really know. Nevertheless, in spite of God's stating *His purpose*, Nettleton chose to use this event to support his own purpose of endorsing election to salvation. He, himself, is proof of the freewill of man. It would be inconceivable that God would direct someone to use Scripture and apply it contrary to the purpose *clearly* stated in His word.

Again, He used the widow woman to sustain His servant, Elijah. He could have chosen anyone, but He happened to choose this woman--NOT TO SALVATION--as this has nothing to do with salvation at all.

The second purpose was to prove to this woman, by the raising of her son from the dead, that Elijah was truly God's prophet. There were many miracles done in the Old and New Testaments, but this had absolutely nothing to do with salvation. Remember, the purpose of the miracle was to convince the woman that Elijah was a true prophet.

Nettleton also uses Luke 4:27 as support of his doctrine of election:

> *"And many lepers were in Israel in the time of Eliseus the prophet; and none of them was cleansed, saving Naaman the Syrian."*

Let us notice the record of this that Christ quoted is found in the Old Testament in 2 Kings 5:3-15. One should take time and read the whole account for themselves. In essence, we find that Naaman was a Syrian and he was a captain of the host of the king of Syria. He was a great man with his master, honorable, and a mighty man in valor but he was a leper, as recorded in 2nd Kings 5:1. We find out how this whole situation took place, how God worked and the *reason* for all of this concerning Naaman, the leper.

God's *purpose* for healing him was *to prove that there was a true God in Israel!* God performed this miracle in healing the leper, to prove to all the company that was with him at that time, that only the true God of Israel could do such a thing. This He did by the prophet, Elisha.

Again we emphasize that this had nothing to do with salvation whatsoever! God performed this miracle to substantiate the fact that there was only one God and that was Israel's JEHOVAH. This was the *purpose* of God.

We find when we read on in the story and let the Scriptures speak for themselves, the purpose of God is made known. In 2 Kings 5:2 we find that the Syrians had gone out by companies and had brought away captive out of the land of Israel a little maid who waited on Naaman's wife. He had taken the girl into his home and she was the maid of the house. She knew that her master was a leper and she told her mistress how he could be cured. The record is found in Verse 3:

> *"....Would God my lord were with the prophet that is in Samaria! for he would recover him of his leprosy."*

This information came to the king of Syria, who sent a letter to the king of Israel, who at that time was Jehoram. When Jehoram got the letter he made the statement, "I'm not God!" It is recorded in Verse 7:

> *"And it came to pass when the king of Israel had read the letter, that he rent his clothes and said, Am I God, to kill and to make alive, that this man doth send unto me to recover a man of his leprosy. Wherefore consider, I pray you..."*

Now when Elisha heard of this he said, "Send the man unto me," and this is exactly what happened. We are told that Naaman came unto the house of Elisha who gave him instructions to follow so his leprosy would be cured. Here is the record found in Verses 9 and 10:

> *"So Naaman came with his horses and his chariot, and stood at the door of the house of Elisha.*

And Elisha sent a message unto him, saying, Go and wash in Jordan seven times, and thy flesh shall come again to thee, and thou shalt be clean."

When Naaman heard this he became very angry because he thought Elisha would just come out of the house and put his hand over him and he would be healed. That is not the way God chose to do it. Notice Verse 13:

"And his servants came near, and spake unto him, and said, my father, if the prophet had bid thee to do some great thing, wouldest thou not have done it? How much rather then, when he saith to thee, wash and be clean?"

They talked him into it and he went down and dipped himself seven times in the Jordan River. The last part of Verse 14 tells us that he was cleansed. Then in Verse 15 the REASON for this is stated:

"And he returned to the man of God, he and all his company, and came, and stood before him: and he said, Behold, now I know that there is no God in all the earth, but in Israel: now, therefore, I pray thee, take a blessing of thy servant."

This was the purpose of God in sending Naaman to his prophet, Elisha. It was to be a testimony by the healing of this man, that God was truly the God of Israel. No idolistic gods could do what the true God had just done.

It taxes my imagination to see someone use these Scriptures to support a false doctrine of electing some to be saved and others to be lost. Again, allow me to quote Nettleton's statement after using these verses in support of his doctrine. (*Chosen to Salvation*, page 26.)

"One out of many widows was chosen, and one out of many lepers was cleansed. The result of such teaching was anger. Special mercy was shown to the widow and to the leper."

37

Also quoting, page 13 and 14 of *Chosen to Salvation*.

"There are two things man will never understand this side of Heaven: how God could elect to save some sinners and not others..."

How important it is to study the Scriptures for yourself. How contradictory Nettleton's applications are to the clear *purpose* of God as stated in His word. Allow me to summarize briefly the purpose of God in each event:

A. Elijah sent to the widow's house.
PURPOSE—*"I have commanded a widow woman there to <u>sustain thee."</u> - 1 Kings 17:9*

B. Elijah restores life to the widow's son.
PURPOSE—*"Now by this I know that thou art a man of God, and that the word of the Lord in thy mouth is truth." - 1 Kings 17:24*

C. Elisha directs Naaman who is healed of leprosy.
PURPOSE—*"...Behold, now I (Naaman) know that there is no God in all the earth, but in Israel..." - 2 Kings 5:15*

The over-all scene is clearly pictured in Luke 4:14 to 29. Christ was raised in Nazareth as a child (Luke 2:39-40). In His ministry, He returned to Nazareth and preached in the synagogue (Luke 4:16). He is telling the Jews that he was anointed to heal the brokenhearted, preach deliverance to the captives and open the eyes of the blind (18). They ask Him to do the same miracles here in Nazareth that they heard He had done in Capernaum. Christ knew they would not believe Him, even if He did them; therefore He stated that *"...No prophet is accepted in his own country* (23,24)." To substantiate this, He uses two Old Testament illustrations, one of Elisha and the other concerning Elijah (25-27). In other words, the same principle was true in Old Testament times as it was in Jesus' day.

"For Jesus himself testified, that a prophet hath no honour in his own country." - John 4:44.

To extract theses two illustrations used by Christ and attempt to make them support the doctrine of election to salvation is asinine! May we always take time to examine the Scriptures for ourselves.

2.   Matthew 20:16. - Not Chosen For Salvation; But, Service!

"So the last shall be first, and the first last: for many be called, but few chosen." -Matthew 20:16.

Now notice Verse 1 of this chapter:

"For the kingdom of heaven is like unto a man that is a householder which went out early in the morning to hire laborers into his vineyard." - Matthew 20:1

This is the "Parable of the Laborers in the Vineyard." We need the context to find out why God said this and to what it is referring. It is not referring to salvation as many try to apply it. In Verse 2, he had gone out into the vineyard:

"And when he had agreed with the laborers for a penny a day, he sent them into his vineyard."

We find out there were others that also went in Verse 7:

"They say unto him, Because no man hath hired us. He saith unto them, Go ye also into the vineyard; and whosoever is right, that shall ye receive."

When it came to the end of the day, we find in Verse 10:

"But when the first came, they supposed that they should have received more; and they likewise received every man a penny."

Notice carefully. Those who murmured had made a deal with God (the Good Man of the house) to work for Him for a certain amount and God had simply kept His part of the bargain. They did not trust God to reward them honestly. What they actually did was limit the grace and goodness of God. God would have given them more. But God gave them exactly what they had agreed to, and that was a penny a day. The others came freely, just trusting that God would reward them accordingly, and He did. Then we come on down and find out at the conclusion of the parable in Verse 16:

"So the last shall be first, and the first last: for many be called, but few chosen."

The Greek word for "called" is "invited or appointed to service." There are only a few chosen and the reason is because of their attitude. Just as this parable reveals--the first who came, came because they made a deal with the Lord. They did not receive the kind of reward that God would have given them if they had not limited God by their dealings.

Therefore, the whole point of this parable is--they are all invited (this being the "many"), but only those are "chosen" who come with the right attitude for service, trusting that God will reward them justly. This is the whole point of the parable. It concerns service and has nothing to do with salvation whatsoever! Many are called, but only a few are chosen for a full reward due to the attitude they take of their own free will. How important it is to examine the context of a parable to determine if that parable is speaking concerning salvation or service.

3. 1 Peter 1:2,3. - Because God Knows The Future Does Not Cancel Out Man's Free Will

"Elect according to the foreknowledge of God the Father, through sanctification of the Spirit, unto obedience and sprinkling of the blood of Jesus Christ: grace unto you, and peace, be multiplied. (2)

Blessed be the God and Father of our Lord Jesus Christ, which according to his abundant mercy hath begotten us again unto a lively hope by the resurrection of Jesus Christ from the dead." - 1 Peter 1:2,3.

In Nettleton's book he quotes 1 Peter 1:2 on page 33, emphasizing "unto obedience." He then goes on to explain what he feels these verses mean, and I quote:

"This matter of salvation is a matter of begetting. In natural physical life the parent begets children: he chooses to have children, follows normal methods and means, and children are born. In the spiritual realm it is much the same. *God decides to have spiritual children and chooses from among the sons of men certain individuals and saves them. That is election. It is a mystery, but a fact to be believed."*

He further goes on in the next paragraph and states:

"It is readily acknowledged that in the spiritual birth the one born makes a choice. He exercises faith, whereas he did nothing in the process of natural birth. Yes, there is a difference between natural birth and spiritual birth, but one truth remains: the choice of the parent plays a part. Physical parents make a choice in the natural birth; God makes a choice in the spiritual birth. We are 'begotten'."

This is Mr. Nettleton's reasoning. The only problem with this is, this is an allegory chosen by Mr. Nettleton and not used by God! To say that God makes a choice as to who goes to Heaven and who does not, would again contradict His Word that He is *"not willing that any should perish"* (2 Peter 3:9). Why did His Son die for the sins of the *world*? Why not just die for the sins of those who have already been elected?

Something that is not brought out in Nettleton's allegory is this--when the children are born and begin to grow, the choice of what avenue of life he wishes to take is left up to the child. He may want to be a doctor, a carpenter, a dentist or whatever profession he chooses. That choice is up to him. The parent may try to make him choose, but still the choice is left up to the child of the natural parent. So it is with each one of us. We have a choice about what we are going to do when we reach the age of accountability concerning Christ. We can either accept or reject Him as our Savior.

Since Nettleton claims election to salvation by stating God made a choice in the spiritual birth--since we are all sinners, on what merit did God make the choice? Of course, he reverts back to the statement that, "It is a mystery!" No, it only becomes a mystery when one accuses God of doing something He did not do. Then--and only then--does it become a mystery and one must hide under this shield because it cannot be explained. Yet, if we take the Word of God so simply, we can explain that God did love the world and that He sent His only begotten Son--that He is not willing any should perish but that all should come to repentance (a change of mind). Now, anyone can understand that!

It is when men begin to use allegories and begin to attempt to extract one verse of Scripture and make it mean what they want it to, that we have to insert the word "mystery" because we cannot understand the position we have taken! It is because of man's philosophy that the so-called "mystery" cannot be understood--not because of the clear teaching of the Word of God. I understand that God knows everything, Christ died for all, He is not willing any should perish, I have a free will and God will honor my decision when I die (Heaven or Hell). Only when man, by his wisdom, thinks he can explain these things better than God, do we find a "mystery" and confusion.

While 1 Peter 1:2,3 is used in support of election to salvation, I would like to continue on into the chapter and, again, let the Scriptures speak for themselves. We find in Verses 8 and 9 that Peter says:

> *"Whom having not seen, ye love; in whom, though now ye see him not, yet believing, ye rejoice with joy unspeakable and full of glory. (8)Receiving the end of your faith, even the salvation of your souls." (9)*

"Your faith" in Verse 9 is possessive. It is your faith…the personal pronoun. Yet we find out it does not say, "Receiving the end of the faith God gave you." It does say, *"Receiving the end of your faith."* You have put your faith in Christ and the end of your faith is, of course, *"the salvation of your souls."*

In Verse 22 we are told:

> *"Seeing ye have purified your souls in obeying the truth through the Spirit unto unfeigned love of the brethren, see that ye love one another with pure heart fervently."*

We do this out of our own free will. In other words, we have the right to obey the truth or to reject the truth of the Word of God.

Then we find that the word of God says, *"See that ye love one another with a pure heart fervently."* Why does Peter give that admonition if you do not have a right to do that or to neglect doing that? He admonishes us, therefore, to do it. He would not do so if we were already elected to love one another with a pure heart fervently, with no choice of our own. There would be no reason for Peter to even bring it to mind if we were elected to do it automatically.

There would be no reason to put all of the exhortations in the New Testament to serve Christ and to urge others to serve Christ. There would be no reason for this whatsoever, if we are elected to service, believing that election over-rides our free will. Why would the Scriptures be asking us to serve Christ? We would just automatically do so.

Of course, this is erroneous and not the teaching of the Word of God. No wonder those who claim election to salvation have to always throw it back as a "mystery" as to the sovereignty of God. Yes, God does know everything about everything. He knows the things that would have happened if the things had not happened that did happen. He knows everything about everything; but, because He knows the end from beginning does not mean that He makes machines out of people. He wants them to "love Him because He first loved us" (1 John 4:19).

4. 1 Peter 5:13. - Elected Because They Had Received Christ

"The church that is at Babylon, elected together with you, saluteth you; and so doth Marcus my son. - 1 Peter 5:13.

Mr. Nettleton uses this portion of Scriptures in support of his position of election to salvation and quotes this portion of Scripture on page 34 of his book. I would like to call your attention to the fact that the church at Babylon, when Scripture states *"was elected together with you,"* was elected as far as being a group of believers in Babylon.

They were elected because they had first received Christ as their Savior. A similar situation occurs when many boys

44

"go out" for a basketball team. Only those that make the team are elected to play the game. We find out that in God's army, only those who choose to put their faith in Christ are elected to be soldiers.

At times Christians are referred to, collectively, as the universal church; or, at times, they are referred to as a church within a local city made up of all believers in that city. At other times they are referred to as an individual Christian. They are referred to as "the elected" only on the basis of their faith in Christ. This is backed up in the same chapter. Notice in Verse 8:

"Be sober, be vigilant; because your adversary the devil, as a roaring lion, walketh about, seeking whom he may devour."

In Verse 9, Peter warns:

"Whom resist steadfast in the faith, knowing that the same afflictions are accomplished in your brethren that are in the world."

Not by election, but by Christ Jesus. And we find out that, *"No man cometh unto the Father, but by me* (John 14:6b)." *"...If I be lifted up from the earth, will draw all men unto me* (John 12:32)." That is through the cross. *"...after that you have suffered a while, make you perfect, established, settle you."* (1 Peter 5:10b)

Notice again in Verse 9, *"Whom resist steadfast in the faith."* That is the responsibility of the believer. No, we are not elected in the sense of God taking away our free will to serve Him. We are told to <u>resist</u>! How do we do this? By choosing to obey the Word of God. Now if we were elected and not going to backslide and have no free will, then why put this warning in the Word of God? One can see that election over-riding man's free will holds no Scriptural foundation whatsoever, because it is built upon man's philosophy and not upon the Word of God.

When 1 Peter 5:10 says that God *"...hath called us unto his eternal glory,"* He tells us how He calls us--*"...by Christ Jesus."* We have a choice, then, to believe or not believe when He calls us by the gospel. In Romans 10:17 we are told:

> *"So then faith cometh by hearing, and hearing by the word of God."*

The Word of God testifies of the death, burial and resurrection of Christ. We have the opportunity to accept it or reject it according to our own free will.

I would like to quote Mr. Nettleton's statements from page 133 of his book. Here we have a classic example of the reverse psychology that he used. Let me quote what he says:

> "It is always helpful to know what others believe. Good and holy people have studied and have stated their findings, their doctrines. Inasmuch as the doctrine of election is a Biblical truth, we profit from studying what good men have stated regarding it. Let me emphasize that these creeds and confessions are not quoted as proof of Bible doctrine, but as proof that good men have held these truths in high esteem."

I hasten to point out--even though men are "good" and "holy" as Mr. Nettleton states, if they hold views contrary to Scripture they are still <u>wrong</u>! And it would seem that if Mr. Nettleton was not going to quote these men as far as proof of Bible doctrine, then why go ahead and quote them at all? This is just a little bit of twisting and reverse psychology that appears to have been used.

46

The statement made by Mr. Nettleton that these confessions and creeds are "proof that good men have held these truths in high esteem" would be of no value unless they were supportive of his position. Then why give them, if it is not to add "clout" to his position? May I point out a case for consideration. In Nettleton's book in support of his position of election to salvation, the following appears:

Pages 51 to 79 contain two sermons by two preachers who support his position.

Pages 87 to 102--eight men are quoted who adhere to his same position.

Pages 105 to 130--under the chapter heading of "Theologian's Statements", six men are quoted.

Pages 133 to 140--under the chapter heading "Confessions of Faith," there are many quotes.

Pages 147 to 157--"A Case In Point, The G.A.R.B.C."

Mr. Nettleton has devoted approximately 88 pages of his book to quoting men and institutions in agreement with his doctrine. It is true, as he says, "Good men do not prove the Bible true." By word Nettleton would justify himself, but by deed he would draw on 88 pages to convince *me by other men's words* that his position is correct. I would have been more interested in 88 pages of his personal exposition of this doctrine instead of the 88 pages he devoted to it in a book of 180 pages. As I attempted to feed on a statement of truth, I found I was digesting a little reverse psychology. The act did not correspond with the words.

There would be no problem filling this book with numerous pages containing theologians, Bible colleges, and etc. that support the position of this author, but it is not my purpose to see who can get the most noted authorities on their side. That is why I have stayed with the Word of God as we examine verses in their context, along with other

Scripture. Then what you choose to believe is based upon God's Word and not that of men, no matter how well known they are.

> *"It is better to trust in the Lord than to put confidence in man."* - Psalm 118:8

5. Matthew 22:14 . - An Earthly Situation Describes A Spiritual Truth. Are You Wearing Your Wedding Garment?

> *"For many are called, but few are chosen."* Matthew 22:14

As we examine this portion of Scripture (Matthew 22) we find in Verses One and Two that this is a parable:

> *"And Jesus answered and spoke unto them again by parables, and said, The kingdom of heaven is like unto a certain king, which made a marriage for his son."*

This parable is used of an earthly situation to illustrate a divine truth. You will notice in Verse 4 that He sent His servants out with the Gospel and instructed them:

> *"...Behold, I have prepared my dinner: my oxen and my fatlings are killed, and all things are ready: come unto the marriage."*

And then in Verse Five:

> *"But they made light of it, and went their ways, one to his farm, another to his merchandise."*

We find out that they treated the servants badly. And then in Verse Nine:

> *"Go ye therefore into the highways, and as many as ye shall find, bid to the marriage."*

"As many as ye find." This is everyone! Everyone you come in contact with.

Verse Ten:

48

"So those servants went out into the highways, and gathered together all as many as they found."

"All" is equivalent to *"as many."* The word *"many"* is used in reference to *"all"* many times in the Bible. Notice, they were to invite both the bad and the good. God is not prejudiced. "The bad" were the ones visibly practicing sin and "the good" were the self-righteous. Both were lost, or both would not have been invited.

We continue and find that some came to the wedding; but, they had to wear wedding garments picturing the righteousness of Jesus Christ. Many came, the bad and the good. The good came in their own righteousness.

Suddenly, in Verse 12 and 13, we see a guest who lacked the proper attire:

"And he saith unto him, Friend, how camest thou in hither not having a wedding garment? And he was speechless. (12)

Then said the king to the servants, Bind him hand and foot, and take him away, and cast him into darkness; there shall be weeping and gnashing of teeth." (13)

So we find that the good came in their own righteousness, and they were rejected. *"Not by works of righteousness which we have done, but according to his mercy he saved us..."* (Titus 3:5). That is what this parable illustrates.

The verse that is used in saying that God called us to salvation is found in the conclusion of this parable. I'll quote the verse again, *"For many are called, but few are chosen."* He is referring to the *"many"* who are also the *"all"* in Verse 10. To gather <u>all</u> or <u>as many</u> as they found. *"As many"* and *"all"* are used interchangeably here for "everyone." Then "Many are called (or all are called) but few are chosen." The *"many"* here are as many as they could come in contact with, but everyone they came in contact with was *"all"* of them so they invited everyone.

You could read this with words used interchangeably, *"For all are called, but few are chosen,"* and only those chosen are chosen on their acceptance of the righteousness of Christ. The others were rejected because they <u>chose</u> to stand before God in their own self-righteousness. This has nothing to do with God choosing to save some and choosing to condemn some, or He would not have called <u>all</u>. This, again, would be mutilation of the Scriptures. Those chosen were chosen on the basis of how they came to the supper and presented themselves, out of their *own free will!*

A good example of the terminology also used is found in Romans 5, where we find the contrast here between "all in Adam die" and "all in Christ are made alive." The important thing is about using the word *"many"* along with *"all"* as used interchangeably here. "Many" does not mean "some to the exclusion of others." "Many" is referring to "all" and we will see that here. Notice in Romans 5:15:

> *"But not as the offense, so also is the free gift: For if through the offense of one many be dead, much more the grace of God, and the gift by grace, which is by one man, Jesus Christ, hath abounded unto many."*

You will find out here that "through the offense, *many* be dead." Notice if you will, as we look down to Verse 18 the contrast continues:

> *"Therefore as by the offense of one (Adam) judgment came upon all men to condemnation."*

So *"all"* and *"many"* are used not contradictory to one another, but complimentary to one another. Just read the rest of the context and this becomes clear.

We find the interchangeability of these words carried on in this passage also concerning Christ. We find in Verse 15 that

> *"...by one man, Jesus Christ (this gift in grace), hath abounded unto many."*

Notice again in Verse 18,

> *"...even so by the righteousness of one the free gift came upon all men unto justification of life."*

So here you have the words *"many"* and *"all"* used interchangeably and both referring to "entirety" or "everyone."

You see, it would be distorting God's word to eliminate *"all"* and say that it means "many except those whom God has predestinated to Hell." This would not be honest with the context of Scripture whatsoever. No, this does not mean in Matthew 22:14 that *"Many are called, but few are chosen"* to salvation. *"All"* are called, this is the word used interchangeably with *"many."* *"Few are chosen"* as only those are chosen that come as a sinner with the righteousness of Christ and not their own righteousness.

> *"For he hath made him to be sin for us, who knew no sin; that we might be made the righteousness of God in him."*
> *2 Corinthians 5:21.*

6. Acts 9:15 - Chosen Or Called For Service. What Can You Do?

> *"But the Lord said unto him, Go thy way: for he is a chosen vessel unto me, to bear my name before the Gentiles, and kings, and the children of Israel."- Acts 9:15.*

These were God's instructions to Ananias to go unto Paul and instruct him. Here we find that Paul was a chosen vessel for *service*! And it says, *"...to bear my name before Gentiles."* It does not say, "You are a chosen vessel to be saved." Paul was a chosen vessel to bear God's name to a specific people, *"before the Gentiles, and kings, and the*

51

children of Israel." God had a specific purpose in mind for the Apostle Paul. That is why you find that Paul begins his Epistles the way he does. For example:

> *"Paul, a servant of Jesus Christ, called to be an apostle, separated unto the gospel of God."- Romans 1:1.*

Not called to *salvation*, called to *be an apostle*! One that was sent with the Gospel of Christ. That is what Paul was called to do. In fact, he stated this in the heading of most of his letters as others were constantly challenging his calling as an apostle. He had to constantly reaffirm it. This is similar to the situation in many churches when men in a church will not accept the authority of the pastor who has been called and placed in that church. Paul had to constantly defend his apostleship as many pastors have to defend their pastor-ship in the church God has led them to and in the position to which He has called them and placed them.

We find in 1 Corinthians 12:12:

> *"For as the body is one, and hath many members, and all the members of that one body, being many, are one body: so also is Christ."*

Paul goes on to liken the body--the foot, the head, the arms, the mouth--to the church or Body of Christ. We find out in Verse 18:

> *"But now hath God set the members every one of them in the body, as it hath pleased him."*

He also says in Verse 11:

> *"But all these worketh that one and the selfsame Spirit, dividing to every man severally as he will."*

Remember--this is for service, not salvation! Going to Verse 6 we find:

"And there are diversities of operation, but it is the same God which worketh all in all."

God does not call all of us to be evangelists nor does He call all of us to be preachers. He does not call us all to be Sunday School superintendents, teachers, choir directors, singers or musicians. But God has called us and given each one of us at least one gift and perhaps more than one.

Here we find in Acts 9:15 that Paul had, very simply, been chosen of God for a specific service. Just as we are a chosen generation and chosen to serve Christ in the particular avenue to which He has led us and for which He has enabled us. We are to covet earnestly the best gift with which to serve Him. Paul was to be an apostle and an evangelist. That was what God had designated him as a "chosen vessel" for--not for salvation. It is unbelievable that those who build their doctrine of election to salvation would use these Scriptures, taking them completely out of context to support their own philosophy.

7. Acts 10:41. - Chosen To Witness; Not Chosen to Salvation!

"Not to all the people, but unto witnesses chosen before of God, even to us, who did eat and drink with him after he rose from the dead." - Acts 10:41.

It is inconceivable that some would use this verse to endorse their doctrine of election, but nevertheless they do. All one has to do is read the context of chapters 10 and 11 and you will find out that this is a meeting that God brought about between Peter and Cornelius, who was a Gentile. In Verse 34 where Peter begins to speak:

"Then Peter opened his mouth, and said, of a truth I perceive that God is no respecter of persons."

Continuing in Verse 35:

53

"...in every nation he that feareth him, and worketh righteousness, is accepted with him."

He then reviews the situation in Verse 39:

"And we are witnesses of all things which he did both in the land of the Jews, and in Jerusalem; whom they slew and hanged on a tree."

We find out here that these are chosen witnesses that Christ would appear to and who would, in turn, testify of His resurrection. It has absolutely nothing to do with salvation. Only that God had elected certain ones to whom Christ would appear first. We find out in 1 Corinthians 15:6 that:

"After that, he was seen of above five hundred brethren at once; of whom the greater part remain unto this present, but some are fallen asleep."

God had selected certain ones to whom He wanted Christ to appear after His resurrection and that <u>only</u> is what the "chosen" in Acts 10:41 is in reference to. They were not chosen for salvation, but to be those to whom Christ should appear after His resurrection.

The amazing thing is that whenever predestinationalists come to the word "chosen" they apply it that God has chosen someone for salvation. There is no way you can get that out of Acts 10:41 even if you stretch the verse from here to China like a rubber band (without it breaking)! A tendency of those who endorse election to salvation whenever they come to the words "chosen", "choosing", or "election" is to do the same thing that *Church of Christ* theologians do when they come to the word "water." They apply it to water baptism! This is the same thing the "election people" do whenever they find the words "chosen" or "election." They will stretch that word a hundred miles out of context to fit it into their man-made doctrine!

54

8. Acts 22:14,15. - Chosen To Be An Apostle; Not Chosen To Salvation!

"And he said, the God of our Fathers hath chosen thee, that thou shouldest know his will, and see that Just One, and shouldest hear the voice of his mouth. (14)

"For thou shalt be his witness unto all men of what thou hast seen and heard." - Acts 22:14,15.

As we examine this we find that we must go back to the 21st Chapter and take the entire context to see what the situation was. In Acts 21:15 we find out that Paul had gone to Jerusalem against the will of the disciples. In Jerusalem we find that he had gone into the temple and the mob came, along with the Roman soldiers, and took him out of the temple. Paul was then called upon to give his testimony. We pick up the story in Verse 38 of Acts 21 as they were trying to find out who Paul was:

"Art not thou that Egyptian, which before these days madest an uproar, and leddest out into the wilderness four thousand men that were murderers? (38) But Paul said, I am a man which am a Jew of Tartus, a city in Cilicia, a citizen of no mean city: and, I beseech thee, suffer me to speak unto the people." - Acts 21:38,39

Then he continues with his testimony of what had happened. Actually, this is just rehearsal of the conversation of the Apostle Paul found in the 9th chapter of Acts. Here in Acts 22, he gives his testimony of how God had dealt with Ananias in sending him to Paul.

"And one Ananias, a devoted man according to the law, having a good report of all the Jews which dwelt there, (12)

Came unto me, and stood, and said unto me, Brother Saul, receive thy sight. And the same hour I looked upon him. (13)

And he said, the God of our fathers hath chosen thee..."
- Acts 22:12-14a.

Notice carefully, the Bible does not say "chosen thee to salvation." This agrees, again, with Acts 9:15:

"...He is a chosen vessel unto me, to bear my name before the Gentiles, and kings, and the children of Israel."

That is what he was chosen for. It does not say anything about "chosen to be saved." *"...chosen...that thou shouldest know his will."* That is what Paul is chosen to do as the Scriptures clearly state:

"...and see that Just One, and shouldest hear the voice of his mouth, For thou shalt be his witness unto all men of what thou hast seen and heard." - Acts 22:14b,15.

As we said, this is only a repeat of Paul's testimony before the people in Jerusalem, rehearsing what actually took place in Acts 9. Again, Acts 9:15 and 16 clearly state:

"But the Lord said unto him, go thy way: for he is a chosen vessel (not for salvation) unto me, to bear my name before the Gentiles, and kings, and the children of Israel. (15)

For I will show him how great things he must suffer for my name's sake." (16)

This is what he was chosen for. As we have said before, he continually had to defend his apostleship. In almost all of his epistles he begins with, "Paul, an apostle of Christ," because that apostleship was not accepted by some of the other disciples and many other men.

9.   Romans 16:13. - Chosen <u>In</u> The Lord; Already Saved

"Salute Rufus chosen in the Lord, and his mother and mine." - Romans 16:13.

Very simply, many times when the word "chosen" is used, it is "chosen in the Lord" for service. God chooses us to serve because of our faithfulness. He wants us to serve Him and, in the context here, Paul is saluting those who have been faithful to serve the Lord. Therefore we find out here that Paul does not "salute Rufus chosen <u>by</u> the Lord, and his mother and mine." Notice, if this portion of Scripture would be referring to salvation it would then read, "chosen <u>by</u> the Lord." But Paul is commenting upon them here with regard to their faithfulness to Christ.

In Verse 6 he says:

"Greet many, who bestowed much labor on us."

And in Verse 7:

"Salute Andronicus and Junia, my kinsmen, and my fellow prisoners (they were also in prison), who are of note among the apostles, who also were in Christ before me."

They were saved prior to Paul. You will find these commendations all through this chapter, as in Verse 3:

"Greet Priscilla and Aquila, my helpers in Christ Jesus: who have for my life laid down their own necks: unto whom not only I give thanks, but also all the churches of the Gentiles."

He comes on down, greeting each one and makes a statement here in Verse 13:

"Salute Rufus <u>chosen in the Lord</u>, and his mother and mine.

As this verse agrees with other Scriptures; therefore, Paul is commending them for their service, not concerning their salvation. I do not see him speaking about anyone's salvation, but complimenting them on their faithfulness after they are saved. I do not know how one could draw any other conclusion than "chosen in the Lord" for service. Rufus was faithful and the Bible does not say, "chosen by the Lord." This agrees with all other Scripture concerning the <u>free will</u> of man in choosing to serve Christ or not to serve Christ.

10. 2 Corinthians 8:19. - Chosen To Travel With Paul; Not Chosen To Salvation!

> *"And not that only, but who was also chosen of the churches to travel with us with this grace, which is administered by us to the glory of the same Lord, and declaration of your ready mind."- 2 Corinthians 8:19.*

When we back up we find out that Paul was writing to the Corinthians and you will see in Verse 16 that the churches chose one to travel as they would support him as a missionary to represent Christ. God did not choose anyone here for salvation. It is hard to believe that this verse is used as a reference in support of election to salvation.

Notice Verse 16, if you will:

> *"But thanks be to God, which put the same earnest care into the heart of Titus for you."*

In other words, God had directed His love into Titus for those in Corinth.

> *"For indeed he accepted the exhortation; but being more forward, of his own accord he went unto you."*

Verse 17 tells us that Titus also had a desire of his own. Verses 18 and 19 continue:

> *"And we have sent with him the brother, whose praise is in the gospel throughout all the churches; (18)*

And not that only, but who was also chosen of the churches to travel with us with this grace..." (19)

Here we find the churches had chosen a brother to travel with Paul. God had nothing to do here with choosing anyone for salvation. It is hard to understand why one would use this verse to support election to salvation. In fact, the Greek word for "chosen" in 2 Corinthians 8:19 is a different Greek word than is usually used for "chosen." It is Greek word "cheirotoneo." It is a combination of two words. It means to be a "hand reacher" or "voter by the raising of the hand." Literally, it means to "select or appoint." So he was selected or appointed by a vote in order to represent the churches and to be sent out by the churches. How in the world anyone could use this as a leverage verse to support election to salvation is beyond me! This is the extreme to which men will go with the Bible in order to prove a man-made doctrine.

11. 2 Timothy 2:4. - Chosen To Be A Soldier; Not Chosen To Salvation!

"No man that warreth entangleth himself with the affairs of this file; that he may please him who hath chosen him to be a soldier." - 2 Timothy 2:4

The verse, itself, is self-explanatory. Paul is simply writing to young Timothy to encourage him to be a good soldier. God has chosen him to be a soldier. It does not say He had chosen him to salvation! In fact, you cannot be a soldier for Christ until you have already received Christ as your personal Savior. The Bible tells us in John 1:12:

"But as many as received him, to them gave he power to become the sons of God, even to them that believe on his name."

Here, writing to young Timothy, he simply states that he "hath chosen him to be a soldier," not to be a Christian as he was already saved. To take 2 Timothy 2:4 as leverage to convince someone that God has either chosen you to be saved or rejected you and ordained you to be lost is absolutely erroneous! Again, the Greek word for "chosen" is a different Greek word than is usually used. It is "stratologeo," and according to my Lexicon it literally means "to gather as a warrior." It is to enlist one into the army, or choose one to be a soldier. It has nothing to do with choosing one for salvation.

12. John 17:2,6,9,11,12, 24. - "Only A Special Limited Group To Be Saved!" A Contradiction To God's Word.

We now go to John, chapter 17. In his book Mr. Nettleton quotes portions of John 17:2,6,9,11,12 and 24. The portions that contain the statements "as many as thou hast <u>given</u> <u>him</u>" or "them which thou hast *given me*" he uses to endorse his position of election to salvation. Then in his book on page 27, his conclusion after quoting portions of each of the foregoing Scriptures is:

> "Christ is the Father's love gift to us. We are the Father's love gift to Christ. 'As many as thou hast given me.' That speaks seven times over of a special, limited group given by the Father to Christ. He planned it and is executing that plan. It is beyond our comprehension, but precious to believe."

Nettleton's position is that only those are going to be saved whom the Father chooses or elects to give to Christ. Of course, the only problem with this interpretation is--it contradicts other portions of God's Word. For example--in the same Gospel, John, we would have a contradiction if we held to this interpretation. In John 3:17 we are told:

> *"For God sent not his Son into the world to condemn the world; but that the world through him might be saved."*

60

How many is the "world?" That is everyone, as it is the Father's will that no one should perish. He sent Christ into the world that through Him the *world* might be saved.

Again, in John 3:16:

> *"For God so loved the world, that he gave his only begotten Son, that whosoever believeth in him should not perish, but have everlasting life."*

Nettleton's interpretation of the verses in John 17 contradicts other portions of God's word and, of course, God cannot contradict Himself! As the Bible says:

> *"...Let God be true, but every man a liar..." Romans 3:4*

Now, concerning the points that Mr. Nettleton stressed in John 17 regarding his position on election. We shall return to the Gospel of John to get the proper interpretation of the Father giving those chosen to Christ.

> *"All that the Father giveth me shall come to me; and him that cometh to me I will in no wise cast out." - John 6:37*

When we go to John 6:44 and 45 we find out who the Father gives:

> *"No man can come to me, except the Father which hath sent me draw him..." (V.44)*

So the ones the Father gives are the ones the Father draws, and how does He draw them? The answer is found in John 6:45:

> *"It is written in the prophets, and they shall all be taught of God. Every man therefore that hath heard, and hath learned of the Father, cometh unto me."*

So the Father draws them by the Word of God--the Word that testifies of the death, burial and resurrection of our Lord. Now they cannot come unless they have heard and we are told in Romans 10:17:

> *"So then faith cometh by hearing, and hearing by the word of God."*

As we go to John 12:32 we find out how God draws those He is going to give to Christ. He draws them by the cross. Let us read John 12:32:

"And I, I be lifted up from the earth, will draw all men unto me."

This is not all men without exception, because not all men are going to be saved, but rather all men without distinction as to race, creed, color, environment, or circumstances. When you allow Scripture to interpret Scripture, you get a correct interpretation. But when man takes ones Scripture and does his own interpreting, you come up with a philosophy that makes God out to be a liar. It makes God appear to contradict Himself; and, then, you find you have a false doctrine.

This is exactly what the pseudo-doctrine of election to salvation does. God is

"...not willing that any should perish, but that all should come to repentance."

God would not contradict Himself in the same Gospel. In John 3:17 He states:

"...but that the <u>world</u> through Him might be saved."

And in John 3:18:

"He that believeth on him is not condemned: but he that believeth not is condemned already..."

God is not willing that any in the world should be lost or God would not have said:

"For God sent not his son into the <u>world</u> to condemn the <u>world</u>..."

...because the world was already condemned,

"...but that the <u>world</u> through him might be saved."

It is God's will--because He loves the world--to see every individual saved. But only those who exercise their own free will and right in accepting Christ as Savior will be the ones that the Father presents to the Son. Therefore He draws them by way of the cross. All that respond to the conviction and drawing of the Holy Spirit through the death, burial and resurrection of Christ, believing in Jesus Christ--will the Father give to the Son as His love gift. Remember, it is your choice--your free will to make that decision!

13. Acts 13:48 - Word Order Makes The Difference!

"And when the Gentiles heard this, they were glad, and glorified the word of the Lord: and as many as were ordained to eternal life believed." - Acts 13:48

This verse is used by Mr. Nettleton in his book on page 28. We would like to quote Mr. Nettleton who goes in great lengths into Greek about the word "ordained." He takes the root which is "tasso" and gives the meaning as "to appoint, arrange, order, ordain or decree." Then he gives the way that the word is used in the New Testament.

Now, we have no quarrel with that, whatsoever, and adhere to the definition of the word as being given correctly. But you will find in a careful study that the translation of the wording of this verse is not properly worded. Let us quote the verse again as the King James Translation records it:

"...And as many as were ordained to eternal life believed."

But if this is the correct order and the wording is correct in the King James Version, then we definitely have a contradiction with other portions of Scripture. But you will find, for example, in 1 John 4:14:

"And we have seen and do testify that the Father sent the Son to be the Saviour of the world."

He could not be the Savior of the world if He ordained only *some* to believe.

"For therefore we both labor and suffer reproach, because we trust in the living God, who is the Saviour of all men, specially of those that believe."- 1 Timothy 4:10

He is the Savior of *all men*, but that is put into reality only to those who will believe on the Lord Jesus Christ.

"And if any man hear my words, and believe not, I judge him not: for I came not to judge the world, but to save the world." - John 12:47

Here the *world* is included again.

You will find that the Greek word for "ordained" is "tasso." It is an idiom which means "a commonly used expression meaning to be classified as those possessing eternal life." Of course, it is the same word translated as "determined" in Acts 15:2 and we find out in *"Vine's Expository Words on the Greek New Testament,"* page 68, paragraph 5, along with other translations, that the verse would be properly worded,

"as many as believed, were ordained unto eternal life."

Or;

"...as many as believed were then appointed unto eternal life."

This would be the correct translation as it agrees with every other Scripture God uses concerning eternal life.

14. John 8:47 - Self-Righteous Lost Sinners Do Not Hear God.

"He that is of God heareth God's words; ye therefore hear them not, because ye are not of God."- John 8:47

In examining the reasoning of the exponents of election concerning this verse, they assert that because the ones spoken of were "not of God"--that is, not chosen by God to believe--

they could not hear God's Word. In other words, it was impossible for them to believe because they were not elected of God to be saved.

Let us examine John 8. Jesus went into the temple in Verse 2 and did not leave the temple until Verse 59. This is important to recognize as we find in Verse 3 He is addressing the scribes and the Pharisees:

> *"And the scribes and Pharisees brought unto him a woman taken in adultery..."*

It is important to recognize that He is addressing the scribes and the Pharisees. These are the self-righteous hypocrites, their character being completely exposed in Matthew 23. Christ revealed to them that He was God in human flesh, their Messiah. Let us notice John 8:24:

> *"I said therefore unto you, that ye shall die in your sins: for if ye believe not that I am he, ye shall die in your sins."*

If they rejected Him as Savior they would; therefore, "die in their sins." Then Christ stated in Verse 45:

> *"And because I tell you the truth, ye believe me not."*

The reason they "believed not" was that they wanted to justify themselves. We find this substantiated in Luke 16:14,15 where we read:

> *"And the Pharisees also, who were covetous, heard all these things: and they derided him (Christ). (14) And he said unto them, ye are they which justify yourselves before men; but God knoweth your hearts..." (15)*

God did not infringe upon their free will. They refused to believe because they were self-righteous and would continue to justify themselves before men. In other words, they were too righteous to need a Savior. We might also point out that it would have been purposeless for Christ to walk to or waste any time with them if they were already elected to be lost. God's will is still that:

"All men should honor the Son (Christ), even as they honor the Father." - John 5:23

All one has to do to find the proper interpretation of John 8:47 is to read the entire eighth chapter of John. Again, may I emphasize the *reason* they "believed not" was because they wanted to *justify themselves.* This was their choice, their free will and the reason behind rejecting Christ. No, God did not elect them to be lost and it is false to say it was impossible for them to believe. God gave them the choice as His will is stated in John 5:23:

"That all men should honor the Son..."

They chose to reject God's will by their own free will.

15. John 10:26-28. - They Were Not "Sheep" As They Believed Not

"But ye believe not, because ye are not of my sheep, as I said unto you. (26), My sheep hear my voice, and I know them, and they follow me: (27) And I give unto them eternal life; and they shall never perish, neither shall any man pluck them out of my hand."- John 10:26-28

Using these verses in support of election, Mr. Nettleton sets forth this reasoning in his book on page 27, and I quote:

"Note the order of words in the verses just quoted. It does not say, 'He that heareth God's words is of God.' It gives the divine side—'He that is of God heareth God's words.'

It does not say, 'Ye are not of my sheep because ye believe not.' Rather it says, 'But ye believe not, because ye are not of my sheep.' "

The problem with this reasoning--as good as it may sound--is that it *contradicts God's word*!

In the same Gospel we find:

66

"And <u>whosoever</u> liveth and believeth in me shall never die. Believest thou this?" - John 11:26

Notice in John 10:6 that Christ spoke this <u>parable</u> to them concerning the sheep. In Matthew 13:10 the disciples asked:

"...why speakest thou unto them in parables?"

Christ answers their question in the following verses and assures us that it was by *their own will* in choosing not to believe, rather than God's imposing His will upon them:

"Therefore speak I unto them in parables: because seeing they see not; and hearing they hear not, neither do they understand. (13)

For this people's heart is waxed gross, and their ears are dull of hearing, and their eyes they have closed; lest at any time they should see with their eyes, and hear with their ears, and should understand with their heart..." Matthew 13:13,15

The Bible does not say that God closed their eyes, but rather that <u>they</u> have closed their <u>own</u> eyes. The choice and responsibility was totally theirs and the reason for their choice of rejecting Christ is plainly stated in John 10:31 and 33:

"Then the Jews took up stones again to stone him." (31)
The Jews answered him, saying, for a good work we stone thee not; but for blasphemy; and because that thou, being a man, <u>makest thyself God</u>." (33)

If "election to salvation" were true, then He would have had to make them think Christ was not God, so they would fulfill His "election to damnation." Do not ask me to believe John 3:16 that...

"...God so loved the world, that he gave his only begotten Son..."

...and then put it into the minds of some people not to believe it, while on the other hand, God gives others---the so-called "elected"--the faith to believe. This would be mutilation of both the Word and the character of God.

At the end of chapter 10, Christ still reasons with the Jews. Notice Verses 37 and 38:

"If I do not the works of my Father, believe me not. (37) But if I do, though ye believe not me, believe the works: that ye may know and believe, that the Fathers is in me, and I in him." (38) - John 10:37,38

If these Jews are supposed to be already excluded by the "doctrine" of election, then why is Christ still reasoning with them to try and get them to believe? Why should He waste the time? Why should we pray for the lost if the elected are going to be saved anyway and the lost to remain lost--what in the world is the use? Thank God, this is not true!

Again the Word of God speaks clearly and plainly for Itself. Notice in Revelation 22:17:

"And the Spirit and the bride say, Come. And let him that heareth say, Come. And let him that is athirst come. And whosoever will, let him take the water of life freely."

When one studies the doctrine of election and choosing--especially after reviewing the writings of many theologians--one may still be left in awe as we are advised that one cannot reconcile the sovereignty of God and the free will of man. This book is written in defense of the sovereignty of God and the free will of man. The two can easily be reconciled and understood, if one allows Scripture to interpret Scripture. Those who endorse that God has chosen some to salvation consistently point out various statements such as:

"God's election is according to His own sovereign purpose. He has not revealed His reasons for such election." (SOURCE: *Chosen to Salvation*, Nettleton).

"There are two things that men will never understand this side of Heaven, how could God elect

68

to save some sinners and not others. And how He could make man responsible for his faith or unbelief. Our minds are too small and too perverted by sin." (SOURCE: Ibid., 14,15).

One author whose book endorses that God has elected some to be saved, turns right around and makes this statement in his book. "This book does not teach election to Hell." This is unbelievable! (SOURCE: Ibid., 19).

The same book endorsing election states, "It seems safe to say that most people who believe in election do not believe in limited atonement." (SOURCE: Ibid., 20).

Then he quotes again, "One died for all.' (2nd Corinthians 5:14). Let that stand, too." (SOURCE: Ibid., 20)

To sum up statements like this in a couple of words, it amounts to nothing more than a whole lot of double-talk! Those who endorse "election to salvation"--which the Scriptures *do not* teach--ask us to accept this false doctrine "by faith." That is , "Just trust that God knows what He is doing when He elects some to be saved and not others."

Their statement is, "How can God elect some to salvation and not others? How can He plan it all and then turn around and hold man responsible? These things must be taken by faith." (SOURCE: *Chosen to Salvation*, Nettleton, pg. 14)

No! We do not accept Nettleton's philosophy by faith, because it is a man-made philosophy that contradicts other portions of God's word. The Bible says that God is "...not willing that any should perish, but that all should come to repentance" (2nd Peter 3:9). If God is not willing that any should perish, then the doctrine of election of some to salvation is against the character and will of God. This philosophy would make God contradict Himself. Yes, if I believe in election to salvation I would definitely have to have faith--and that faith would have to be in man's teaching, not the Word of God.

16. John 6:37,39. - Christ Draws Men By The Cross.

"All that the Father giveth me shall come to me; and him that cometh to me I will in no wise cast out. (37)

And this is the Father's will which hath sent me, that of all which he hath given me I should lose nothing, but should raise it up again at the last day." John 6:37,39

In reference to these two verses, Mr. Nettleton makes the statement:

"Throughout John 6 the divine side is spoken of along with the human side. Man must believe and God has planned."

Now, I do not know where to find his statement in John 6; nevertheless, these two verses are used to support it. You can make any passage mean what you want it to, if you take two verses and isolate them without taking other verses in the Word that shed light upon these verses. When we come to John 6:37 we find that:

"All that the Father giveth me shall come to me; and him that cometh to me I will in no wise cast out."

Nettleton's comment is this:

"Believers are given to Christ by the Father and such as are given shall come." (Page 26, *Chosen to Salvation*.)

In other words, they do not have any choice, according to Nettleton.

In Verse 39 we read:

"And this is the Father's will which hath sent me, that of all which he hath given me I should lose nothing, but should raise it up again at the last day."

Their reasoning is--all that the Father has given Christ have no choice. They have to come--they will come--and the free will of man is taken away because they must believe. God will even give them the faith to do it with! Therefore, they

70

conclude that man is elected to salvation. "Don't ask us why," the election people say, "because you have to take it by faith. It is all contained in the sovereignty of God and His ways are past finding out! We will never know His ways," and all of that mumbo-jumbo! This is not the teaching of the Word of God.

Let us examine John 6:37 and 39 in their context as we read the rest of the chapter, especially Verses 44 and 45:

> *"No man can come to me (Christ), except the Father which hath sent me draw him: and I will raise him up at the last day." (44)*

> *"It is written in the prophets, and they shall be all taught of God. Every man therefore that hath heard, and hath learned of the Father, cometh unto me." (45)*

We find a little more information that Mr. Nettleton did not include in his writings. Just taking two verses and not using the rest of the chapter or the rest of the Gospel of John would not be consistent with the basic fundamentals of Biblical interpretation. Notice again in John 6:44:

> *"No man can come to me, except the Father which hath sent me draw him: and I will raise him up at the last day."*

The Father is going to have to draw men, and how will He draw them? In John 12:32 the Bible answers for itself:

> *"And I (Christ), if I be lifted up from the earth (the cross) will draw all men unto me."*

The drawing of all men unto Him is through the cross--by the death, burial and resurrection of Christ. Drawing all men is not all men without exception, as we have said; but, rather, all men without distinction as to race, color, or creed. No--God loves the world and gave His only begotten Son in sacrifice for it. To take just two verses (as Mr. Nettleton has done with John 6:37 and 39) and not correlate any other verses in the Gospel of John that speak on the same subject is shown to be erroneous when we find that <u>all</u> men are drawn by the cross. So you see, it <u>is</u> God's will that all should come and be saved.

This is a far cry from seeing the Scriptures twisted and turned, pulling out two verses of Scripture and disregarding the rest of the chapter as well as the rest of the Gospel of John. Is it any wonder a person can make the Bible mean what they want it to when they do not let Scripture interpret Scripture? No--you and I are not one of those who are elected to be saved nor one of those who are elected to be lost.

We have a free will and our destiny is really in our own hands. If you choose to accept the record God has given of His Son, then you will be saved. If you choose to reject the Lord Jesus Christ as your Savior, then the responsibility is yours, as you will spend eternity separated from God. But thanks be to God we have the free will to make that choice and stand responsible for the choice we make!

17. John 6:65,66.- Drawing By The Cross = Drawing By The Gospel.

"And he said, Therefore said I unto you, that no man can come unto me, except it were given him of my Father. (65)

From that time many of his disciples went back, and walked no more with him." - John 6:65,66

One must remember that the Bible is here talking about disciples who were saved and lost. People in both conditions are present. Because the Bible says "disciples" does not mean they were all saved. The word "disciple" means "one that follows" and there were people who followed Christ from place to place--some were sincere and some were just spectators.

72

Mr. Nettleton quotes Verses 65 and 66 in support of his position of "election to salvation" on page 26 of his book. These verses are again easily explained by comparing one Scripture with another as we have previously done. Let us recapitulate. The Bible speaks for itself in John 12:32 and states:

> *"And I (Christ), if I be lifted up from the earth, will draw all men unto me."*

We find out, as before, that the Father draws men through the death, burial and resurrection of Christ. God gave His Son (Christ) to die upon the cross for all. Therefore, it is the Father's will for all to believe on His Son as the Father draws them by the cross. How sad it is to see people reject the free gift of salvation when the price has been completely paid for all.

Let us continue our examination of chapter 6 as we find in Verse 54:

> *"Whoso eateth my flesh, and drinketh my blood, hath eternal life; and I will raise him up at the last day."*

Then in John 6:51:

> *"I am the living bread which came down from Heaven: if any man eat of this bread, he shall live forever: and the bread that I will give is my flesh, which I will give for the life of the world."*

"Any man, world, and *whoso"* in Verse 54, perfectly go together in letting Scripture interpret Scripture. The free will of man is not limited nor infringed upon by the sovereignty of God. We do not have to put in a doctrine that makes man a robot, allowing him no right to make a choice. To say that man will only do as God has elected him to do is erroneous to the true teachings of the word of God!

I am glad God gave us the *whole* Gospel of John. Comparing Scripture with Scripture brings into focus the error of pulling one Scripture out of context and isolating it to fit a man-made doctrine. As we said, this exactly what *Church of Christ* theologians do with John, Chapter 3, concerning the word "water." They apply it to water baptism and disallow Scripture to interpret Scripture. They say in John 3:5 that:

> *"...Except a man be born of water and of the Spirit, he cannot enter into the kingdom of God."*

Then they define the word "water" as literal water. Yet-- if we let the Word of God interpret Itself, we find out that water is used as the cleansing agent as far as salvation is concerned. If we read on in John 3 we find that "water" is used in reference to the Word of God. In John 3:5 the word *"water"* is referring to God's Word. The end result is the same as John 3:16 where "believing in Christ" results in "everlasting life." *"Everlasting life"* is equivalent to *"entering the Kingdom of God."* "Believing" is believing the Word of God, which is represented by the "water." In the same Gospel (15:3) we are told:

> *"Now ye are clean through the word which I have spoken unto you."*

Also in Ephesians 5:26 we find that God shall cleanse His church...

> *"...with the washing of water by the word."*

As we allow Scripture to interpret Scripture, we find out that it is believing the Word of God which is metaphorically referred to here as *"water." "Except a man be born of water and of the Spirit ..."* or "born of the Word."

When we find the words *"born again"* we can go to 1 Peter 1:23 and by letting Scripture interpret Scripture the Bible will tell us what "born again" means:

> "Being born again, not of corruptible seed, but of
> incorruptible, by the word of God, which liveth and abideth
> for ever."

Those who support "election to salvation" make the same
error as the *Church of Christ* theologians. They extract one
Scripture out of context and apply it to their own doctrine. If
we compare one Scripture with another--as they will always
agree--then we have the proper interpretation and the truth as
to God's Word and will.

18. Romans 9:7-13. - When And Why Was Esau Hated?

> *"Neither, because they are the seed of Abraham, are they
> all children: but, In Isaac shall thy seed be called. (7)*
>
> *That is, They which are the children of the flesh, these
> are not the children of God: but the children of the promise
> are counted for the seed. (8)*
>
> *For this is the word of promise, At this time will I come
> and Sarah will have a son. (9)*
>
> *And not only this; but when Rebecca also had conceived
> by one, even by our father Isaac; (10)*
>
> *(For the children being not yet born, neither having done
> any good or evil, that the purpose of God according to
> election might stand, not of works, but of him that calleth;
> (11)*
>
> *It was said unto her, the elder shall serve the younger.
> (12)*
>
> *As it is written, Jacob have I loved, but Esau have I
> hated." - Romans 9:7-13*

As we read these verses we find out that God was electing or choosing (by selective breeding) a nation for Himself. Even though within that nation not everyone would be looking for the coming of Christ; nevertheless, He was selectively breeding a people that would be known as the nation of Israel. God exercised His own choice as to who would be the father of the nation.

When it came to the promise to Abraham and Sarah, God had promised them a son. Of the children they were to have, God would <u>choose</u> through which one the <u>seed</u> and the <u>promise</u> should come. God promised the seed by Abraham and Sarah in Genesis 15:3,4. Too impatient to wait on God's promise, Abraham went unto Hagar who was Sarah's Egyptian handmaid. She conceived and bore a son by the name of Ishmael. But this was not the <u>promised</u> seed through which the nation of Israel should be born.

We find out that later--at a very old age (Abraham being 100 years old and Sarah being 90)--that god fulfilled His promise and Isaac was born (Genesis 21:1-5).

We find that God had said:

"But my covenant will I establish with Isaac..."

God had selected him. This has nothing to do with the salvation of Isaac!

As we continue, we find that Isaac married Rebekah and they had two sons, Jacob and Esau. If you will notice carefully, God had said:

"The elder shall serve the younger."

We find this in Genesis 25:23. This was only to establish the birthright and the ancestral headship of the nation and had absolutely nothing to do with salvation! God had the right to choose through which individual the nation the nation of Israel would be born. But because of that, it does not mean that Esau could have not been saved. In fact, this leads us to the

76

very next point. Those who say you are chosen to salvation miss the point of this message altogether...

> *"As it is written, Jacob have I loved, but Esau have I hated." - Romans 9:13*

Notice carefully, the Bible says "As it is written..." Where do you find this written? Turn with me to Malachi 1:1-3 and this is where it is written. This was never written before Jacob and Esau were born. God did not elect one to be saved and the other to be lost. He did not say "Jacob have I loved, but Esau have I hated" prior to Jacob and Esau's birth. This was said some 1500 years later, after Esau had chosen to practice his evil acts. Then God said, *"Jacob have I loved, but Esau have I hated."*

Remember--this was not done before they were born! It was not God's will to hate Esau before he was ever born! He only chose Jacob as the seed through which the Messiah would come and as an ancestral head in building the lineage of the nation of Israel.

Let us read in Malachi 1:1-3:

> *"The burden of the word of the Lord to Israel by Malachi. (1)*
>
> *I have loved you, saith the lord. Yet ye say, wherein hast thou loved us? Was not Esau Jacob's brother? saith the Lord: yet I loved Jacob. (2)*
>
> *And I hated Esau, and laid his mountains waste for the dragons of the wilderness." (3)*

Notice carefully that God had done what he had said in Malachi. But this was done only after Esau had practiced the evil things and despised his heritage. Most certainly did God do what He said! But God did not say this before Esau was born nor does it relate to his salvation.

God has said to us before we were born:

77

"For God so loved the world, that he gave his only begotten Son, that whosoever believeth on him should not perish, but live an everlasting life." - John 3:16

But after we reject Christ in this life---God hates all workers of iniquity. He assuredly does! But then, we are going to find out that God will honor our choice. It is your choice. Whether you accept or reject Christ, God will honor that choice. If you choose to reject Christ, you will spend eternity in the Lake of Fire. If you choose to accept Christ, you will be passed from death unto life. But it is your choice, because God is...

"not willing that any should perish." - 2 Peter 3:9

Another thing we might notice here is that while this portion of Scripture occurs in the New Testament, it is written almost 400 years after Malachi's words. So there are actually about 1500 years between Verse 12 and Verse 13 of the 9th chapter of Romans. How important it is to take time and to study these Scriptures pertaining to Esau!

Another portion of Scripture concerning Esau is found in Hebrews 12:16,17:

"Lest there be any fornicator, or profane person, as Esau, who for one morsel of meat sold his birthright. (16)

For ye know that afterward, when he would have inherited the blessing, he was rejected: for he found no place of repentance, though he sought it carefully with tears." (17)

We find concerning Esau in Verse 16, "Lest there be any fornicator, or profane person...". The word "profane" here actually means "outside the temple or *worldly.*" He was a worldly person and a fornicator. This describes him "...who for one morsel of meat sold his birthright. For ye know how that afterward, when he would have inherited the blessing..." This is not speaking of eternal life at all! This is speaking of *inheriting the blessing* as far as the headship of the nation is concerned. Again--nothing is said of salvation, whatsoever!

Then we find that "...he found no place of repentance, though he sought it carefully with tears." The word "repentance" is the Greek word "metanoia." Concerning this verse, *"Vine's Expository Words on the Greek New Testament"* has this to say:

> "The word means afterthought or change of mind and is used of repentance from sin or evil. A change of mind about sin or evil. Except in Hebrews 12:17 where the word "repentance" seems to mean not simply a change of Esau's mind but such a change as would reverse the effects of his own previous state of mind. Esau's birth bargain could not be recalled, it involved an irretrievable loss."

Esau was simply sorry to the point of tears, but he did not change his mind about what he had done in forfeiting the blessing he would have inherited.

Again--this has nothing to do with Esau's salvation. Remember this--that there are some 1500 years between Verses 12 and 13 of Romans 9. Malachi had stated that God had loved Jacob and hated Esau after Esau had done these evil things. After he had shown himself to be a profane person and was a fornicator, then God said, "...Esau have I hated." But we find out that God's electing Jacob was only for the blessings that had to do with the headship of the nation of Israel and had <u>nothing</u> <u>to</u> <u>do</u> <u>with</u> <u>salvation</u>!

Proof of Hebrews 12:16 and 17 is found in Genesis 26:34 and 35:

> *"And Esau was forty years old when he took to wife Judith the daughter of Beeri the Hittite, and Bashemath the daughter of Elon the Hittite: (34) Which were a grief of mind unto Isaac and to Rebekah." (35)*

You see, Esau loved worldly women and he should not have taken up a marriage with those that were outside of Israel. He should not have done that, but he loved the worldly women. This is why Hebrews states that he was a fornicator. In Hebrews 12:15 we are told:

> "Looking diligently lest any man fail of the grace of God; lest any root of bitterness springing up trouble you, and thereby many be defiled."

This could surely be descriptive of Esau.

Now notice in Romans 9:15 where God says to Moses:

> "...I will have mercy on whom I will have mercy, and I will have compassion on whom I will have compassion."

This "have mercy" is not referring to the mercy of salvation that God shows to all sinners, but rather the mercy that God had on Esau allowing him to live as long as he did while living a sinful life.

Also speaking of "mercy" in Romans 9:15, we would like to go to Exodus 33 where this is recorded in Verse 19. "Where he saith to Moses." Let us read the record and see what mercy he is talking about back here. We pick up the story in Exodus 33:18:

> "And he said, I beseech thee, shew me thy glory."

This was Moses speaking to God. Then God answers in Verses 19 and 20.

> "And he said, I will make all my goodness pass before thee, and I will proclaim the name of the LORD before thee: and will be gracious to whom to whom I will be gracious, and will shew mercy on whom I will shew mercy. (19)
> And he said, Thou canst not see my face: for there shall no man see me, and live." (20) - Exodus 33:19,20

We find out that God allowed His glory to pass by the cleft of the rock, etc. The point we would like to make is that the mercy that God speaks of is that...

"I... will be gracious unto whom I will be gracious, and will shew mercy to whom I will shew mercy," - Exodus 33:19

This is the fact that God is saying, "I am the One who will determine whether or not I will show you my glory." This had nothing to do with the salvation of Moses at all--neither did it have anything to do with the salvation of Esau. This was God's answer as far as adhering to the request of Moses, and again, it had nothing to do with salvation at all.

It is amazing how many times one will take Scripture and apply it to their man-made philosophical doctrine instead of taking what the Scriptures specifically teach. If those who use Romans 9 would only go back to where it was spoken to Moses and find out what it was spoken concerning, there would be no problem understanding what these Scriptures are speaking about.

<u>Again</u>, this is not speaking about Moses' salvation, but only God's mercy in granting Moses' request to see His glory.

Continuing in the book of Romans, in 9:22 we have the situation concerning Esau summarized. In Verse 22 we are told...

"What if God, willing to shew his wrath, and to make his power known, endured with much longsuffering (I am sure God was very longsuffering with Esau.) the vessels of wrath fitted to destruction."

You see Esau was the type of man who was fitted for destruction by living a sinful life. But God in His longsuffering (this includes the mercy that God extends), even though the individual is undeserving, God extends it to them anyway. This is the supreme "agape" love of God which is far superior to the brotherly "phileo" love of man.

19. Romans 9:17 - Pharaoh, Raised Up For God's Purpose; But, With A Free Will

Here, mighty Pharaoh is used as an illustration.

> *"For the scripture saith unto Pharaoh, Even for this same purpose have I raised thee up, that I might shew my power in thee, and that my name might be declared throughout all the earth."*

We pick up the record of Pharaoh back in the first few chapters of Exodus. We are going to find out that Pharaoh was a very wicked man who had already hardened his heart many, many years concerning the nation of Israel. God also had raised this man up, no doubt, and given him the position that he had.

This did not mean when the Scriptures say " raise him up" that this man did not have a free choice, because he did. You will find that the Bible says that God sets one up in authority and takes down another (Psalms 75:6,7 and Daniel 2:21).

> *"And he changeth the times and the seasons; he removeth kings, and setteth up kings; he giveth wisdom unto the wise, and knowledge to them that know understanding."*
> - Daniel 2:21

You see, God had worked the circumstances out so Pharaoh would be the king of the nation of Egypt. But Pharaoh's choice as to whether he would harden his heart or not was entirely up to him. This man had already hardened his heart many times against the nation of Israel.

Israel had gathered the bricks and gathered their own straw at Pharaoh's command (Exodus 5:8-11). They were slaves in the land at the hand of Pharaoh. He was a very evil, wicked man who had already hardened his heart.

Then it came time for God to lead the nation of Israel out from the bondage of Egypt by the hand of Moses, His servant. Moses, therefore, went unto Pharaoh to carry out the demands that God had made concerning this and challenged Pharaoh. The beginning of the record is found in Exodus 5:1,2:

> *"And afterwards Moses and Aaron went in, and told Pharaoh, Thus saith the Lord God of Israel, Let my people go, that they may hold a feast unto me in the wilderness. (1)*
>
> *And Pharaoh said, Who is the Lord, that I should obey his voice to let Israel go? I know not the Lord, neither will I let Israel go." (2)*

Then we find in Exodus 4:21:

> *"And the Lord said unto Moses, when thou goest to return unto Egypt, see that thou do all those wonders before Pharaoh, which I have put in thine hand: but I will harden his heart, that he shall not let the people go."*

This has confused many, many Christians. They say, "Well, God had hardened Pharaoh's heart. Does that mean he did not have a free will as far as letting the people of Israel go?" No, not at all. We find out that *Pharaoh hardened his own heart* and that God also hardened his heart only by forcing Pharaoh to openly declare his decision. This was done in response to God's command, "Let my people go." We know Pharaoh's heart concerning his treatment of Israel, but we did not know his heart was hardened concerning the freedom of Israel from bondage. God hardened his heart only in the sense of forcing him to make a decision in this matter. Then his heart was hardened only because of the Word of God that had confronted him.

In that sense--God hardened Pharaoh's heart concerning this decision of letting Israel go. I might point out again, this had nothing to do with the salvation of Pharaoh. The hardening of Pharaoh's heart in Romans 9 was concerning letting the nation of Israel out of bondage from the land of Egypt.

God simply pressed the matter to a conclusion and forced Pharaoh to make a decision. In that manner God hardened Pharaoh's heart...or made Pharaoh openly declare his refusal to obey God's command.

We come now to Exodus 8:15:

> "But when Pharaoh saw that there was respite, <u>he hardened his heart</u>, and hearkened not unto them; as the Lord had said."

We find that Pharaoh hardened his heart again. This is in response to Verses 5,12-15:

> "And the Lord spake unto Moses, Say unto Aaron, Stretch forth thine hand with thy rod over the streams, over the rivers, and over the ponds, and cause frogs to come up upon the land of Egypt. And they did so. (5)

> And Moses and Aaron went out from Pharaoh: and Moses cried unto the Lord because of the frogs which he had brought against Pharaoh. (12)

> And the Lord did according to the word of Moses; and the frogs died out from the houses, out of the villages, and out of the fields. (13)

> And they gathered them together upon heaps: and the land stank. (14)

> But when Pharaoh saw there was respite, <u>he hardened his heart,</u> and hearkened not unto them; as the Lord had said." (15)

Here we find out that Pharaoh hardened his own heart (7:13). It was only in the respect that God forced him to make a decision that God hardened Pharaoh's heart. God just pushed the matter to a conclusion. The free will was Pharaoh's! Again, the point we would like to make is that this had nothing to do with Pharaoh's salvation whatsoever.

Mr. Nettleton uses these verses to support his position concerning election on pages 30 and 31 of his book, but neglected to take his readers back to Exodus and show them what Romans was referring to when quoting these men as an example. Pharaoh surely fulfills Proverbs 29:1 where we are told:

> *"He, that being often reproved hardeneth his neck, shall suddenly be destroyed, and that without remedy."*

In Ecclesiastes 9:12 we are told:

> *"For man also knoweth not his time: as the fishes that are taken in an evil net, and as the birds that are caught in the snare; so are the sons of men snared in an evil time, when it falleth suddenly upon them."*

This is exactly what happened to Pharaoh when he pursued the nation of Israel into the Red Sea and God drowned him there with his whole army. He surely had no idea that the time had come when God would render His judgment. He was surely a "vessel fitted to destruction" and a "vessel of wrath." God did not make him that way, as his decisions were of his own free will.

If Pharaoh had no free will you end up with this conclusion--God ordered Pharaoh to free the nation of Israel while at the same time preventing him from doing so. Why would God ask Pharaoh to do something He had no intention of letting him do? This false doctrine makes the God I worship a God of confusion. No--the confusion is the product of false doctrine and those that put it forth, not caused by God.

When God commanded Pharaoh to do something, God extended to him the free will to obey or disobey. No--God is not some demented, deranged psychological being saying one thing and doing another. He is omniscient, omnipotent and His acts and actions are in accordance with His Word (the Bible) and His attributes.

God raised Pharaoh up and showed that He was more powerful than even the mighty king of Egypt! But Pharaoh had a choice. He could have been saved. God loved him, but he hardened his own heart, refusing obedience to God.

The power of God and the wrath of God was shown to be mightier than even this great king. He not only did that to show His wrath upon the vessel fitted to destruction, but He also showed proof to the nation of Israel that no man, no matter what position he held, could ever stand under the hand of God Almighty!

It was an encouragement to the nation of Israel--showing them that whatever they faced in the land of Canaan God could overthrow. If God could destroy the mighty king of Egypt, then they could trust Him to destroy any other king they might face on their march to the land God had graciously promised Abraham, Isaac, and Jacob.

Let us go on and examine Verses 20 and 21 of Romans 9:

> *"Nay, but, O man, who art thou that repliest against God? Shall the thing formed say to him that formed it, why hast thou made me thus? (20)*
>
> *Hath not the potter power over the clay, of the same lump to make one vessel unto honour, and another unto dishonour?" (21)*

One must simply remember that in God's sovereignty He has the right to place any person in the place of honor in the eyes of men without explaining to us the reason. Many times God does tell us His reason for doing so, as he did concerning Pharaoh in Verse 17:

> *"For the scripture saith unto Pharaoh, even for this same purpose have I raised thee up, that I shew my power in thee, and that my name might be declared throughout all the earth."*

86

Again, may I remind our readers that this has nothing to do with the salvation that God has offered by His grace to *everyone.*

Notice in Psalms 75:6,7 where God says:

> *"For promotion cometh neither from the east, nor from the west, nor from the south. But God is the judge: he putteth down one and setteth up another."*

We find that God does raise up certain ones to a position of honor, even if they are lost. He raised up Pharaoh of Egypt, Nebuchadnezzar of the Babylonians, Alexander the Great of the Grecian Empire, Cyrus of the Persian Empire, Antiochus Epiphanes, even Herod the Great. He put these men in a place of position and did show His mercy unto these men even while they hated Him for such a long time. God was not obligated to do so, but He did. God could have killed them at any time, but did extend His mercy to those who were fitted for destruction.

This is just simply God running things the way He wants to run them. God has determined the 1,000-year Reign of Christ. Who determined that? God did. He has prepared the Lake of Fire for the Devil and his angels. Things of this sort are things that God has planned. This is God exercising His sovereign will.

When it comes to God's creation, God says He loved the world. And the fact is, when He says He loved the world, He means He loved the world! He gave His only begotten Son that whosoever, the whosoever goes along with the personal responsibility of everyone and it corresponds with God's loving everyone. He gave His Son for everyone, not just the elect.

Therefore, anyone who wills may come to Christ, believing that He died to pay for their sins and God will give to them eternal life. This is God's will for all; therefore, God would have to go against His own will if election to salvation were true. This would be absolutely impossible.

87

20. Ephesians 1:4 - God's Children Should Walk In Righteousness

"According as he hath chosen us in him before the foundation of the world, that we should be holy and without blame before him in love." - Ephesians 1:4

As we examine this portion of Scripture we find the verse is really self-explanatory. The Christian has been chosen to do something and that something is to lead a righteous life as a testimony. The last part of the verse clarifies this:

"...that we should be holy and without blame before him in love."

This is in perfect accordance with God's Word and is substantiated by Ephesians 2:10. In Ephesians 2:8,9 we are told about salvation:

"For by grace are ye saved through faith; and that not of yourselves: it is the gift of God: Not of works, lest any man should boast."

Now God's will for us after we are saved, as set forth in Verse 8 and 9, is revealed in Verse 10:

"For we are his workmanship, created in Christ Jesus unto good works, which God hath before ordained that we should walk in them."

In order to make Ephesians 1:4 support "election to salvation" one would have to do away with the last part of this verse. But when you compare Scripture with Scripture concerning the same subject, they will always complement one another. Just as Ephesians 2:10 complements Ephesians 1:4.

Very simply, God's will, even before the foundation of the world, was that every Christian should walk the Christian life. To use this verse to support God's choosing only some to be saved would contradict other portions of His Word.

For example, if we say that Ephesians 1:4 is supportive of electing some to be saved, we find it would not agree with John 1:7,12:

> "The same came for a witness, to bear witness of the Light, that all men through him might believe. (7)
>
> But as many as received him, to them gave he power to become the sons of God, even to them that believe on his name." (12)

You see Paul admonished young Timothy in 2 Timothy 2:15 to...

> "Study to shew thyself approved unto God, a work-man that needeth not to be ashamed, rightly dividing the word of truth."

If one simply seeks the truth of God's Word, they will always gather the Scriptures that speak concerning a certain subject and compare them. When they agree and complement each other, then you have the proper interpretation and correct doctrine. The doctrine of "election to salvation" cannot be supported by Ephesians 1:4, as this verse and Ephesians 2:10 are complimentary--revealing God's will, before ordained, that His children should walk in righteousness.

21. 2 Thessalonians 2:13,14 - Called By The Gospel = Drawn By The Cross

> " But we are bound to give thanks alway to God for you, brethren beloved of the Lord, because God hath from the beginning chosen you to salvation through sanctification of the Spirit and belief of the truth: (13) Whereunto he called you by our gospel, to the obtaining of the glory of our Lord Jesus Christ." - 2 Thessalonians 2:13,14

You see, predestinationalists are as excited over the words "chosen" and "election" as the *Church of Christ* are over water! They will swim through rivers, lakes and oceans of grace, faith and free will to stop at a rill of baptism and election for salvation. One would have to throw out the last half of Verse 13 and all of Verse 14 in order to "squeeze out" the doctrine of "election to salvation." On page 33 of Mr. Nettleton's book, *Chosen To Salvation*, he comments upon these verses by saying:

"God decides to have spiritual children and chooses from among the sons of men certain individuals and saves them. This is election. It is a mystery, but a fact to be believed."

"A fact to be believed" *only* if you disregard the Bible. Now notice that the believer is chosen to salvation on the basis of two things:

1. One of them is God's part: *"...through sanctification of the spirit."*

2. The other is man's responsibility. *"...belief of the truth."*

Verse 14 tells us how we are called,

"Whereunto he called you by our gospel, to the obtaining of the glory of our Lord Jesus Christ."

The Gospel is the death, burial and resurrection of Christ and it is by this that He calls all to be saved. Notice again in John 12:32:

"And I (Christ), if I be lifted up (crucified on the cross) from the earth, will draw all men unto me."

In John 4:42 it is made clear that His will is to see everyone saved:

"...for we have heard him (Christ) ourselves, and know that this is indeed the Christ, the Saviour of the world."

90

If we would read all of 2 Thessalonians 2, we would find that this is speaking of the 7-year Tribulation Period when after the 3 1/2 years the Anti-Christ exalts himself in the Jewish Temple and declares himself to be God (Verse 4). Then in Verse 10, those that perish do so because of a decision they make. Verse 10:

> "And with all deceivableness of unrighteousness in them that perish; because they received not (i.e., they would not believe) the love of the truth, that they might be saved."

Then in Verse 11 and 12 God states He will send "The lie." This is the Anti-Christ whom they will believe since they willfully rejected the truth. Notice Verses 11 and 12:

> "And for this cause God shall send them strong delusion, that they should believe a lie: (11) That they all might be damned who believed not the truth, but had pleasure in unrighteousness." (12)

Remember, Christ died for the sins of the <u>world</u>, therefore everyone is invited to come and believe in Christ. John made it perfectly clear that "whosoever" may come. Notice in John 11:25 and 26:

> "Jesus said unto her, I am the resurrection, and the life: he that believeth in me, though he were dead, yet shall he live: and whosoever liveth and believeth in me shall never die. Believest thou this?"

22. James 2:5. - Chosen Because They Were "Rich In Faith"

> "Hearken, my beloved brethren, Hath not God chosen the poor of this world rich in faith, and heirs of the kingdom which he hath promised to them that love him?" - James 2:5

It taxes the imagination that this verse is used to support the doctrine of "election to salvation", but nevertheless, it is by some. The context of Verses 1 to 9 of this chapter is concerning the respect of certain people because of their position. Notice in Verses 2 and 3:

> *"For if there come into your assembly a man with a gold ring, in goodly apparel, and there come in also a poor man in vile raiment; (2) And ye have respect to him that weareth the gay clothing, and say unto him, Sit thou here in a good place; and say to the poor, Stand thou there, or sit here under my footstool:" (3)*

They were judging a person by their possessions, showing favoritism to the rich and despising the poor.

Notice again Verses 6 and 7:

> *"But ye have despised the poor. Do not rich men oppress you, and draw you before the judgment seats? (6) Do not they blaspheme that worthy name by the which ye are called?" (7)*

Verse 5 says <u>why</u> He has chosen the poor:

> *"...Hath not God chosen the poor of this world rich in faith, and heirs of the kingdom which he hath promised to them that love him."*

If these verses were in support of "election to salvation," then <u>all</u> the poor would be saved or else God would be contradicting Himself. Then God would be guilty of the same wrong judgment that He was rebuking some of the Christians for exercising. This would be preposterous!

The verse is self-explanatory and in perfect context with Verses 1 to 9. They were chosen because they were *"rich in faith,"* and *"heirs of the kingdom"* which God had promised to those that love Him. God chooses or rejects all humanity depending on *their faith.* Notice in Hebrews 11:6:

> *"But without faith it is impossible to please him: for he that cometh to God must believe that he is, and that he is a rewarder of them that diligently seek him."*

Now John says that it is the will of God that all should honor the Son. Notice John 5:22 and 23:

> *"For the Father judgeth no man, but hath committed all judgment to the Son: (22) That all men should honour the Son, even as they even as they honour the Father. He that honoureth not the Son honoureth not the Father which hath sent him." (23)*

One of the basic principles of Biblical interpretation is comparing Scripture with Scripture. When this is done, the doctrine of "election to salvation" quickly vanishes.

23. 1 Corinthians 2:14 - What The Natural Man Cannot Know

> *"But the natural man receiveth not the things of the Spirit of God: for they are foolishness unto him: neither can he know them, because they are spiritually discerned." - 1 Corinthians 2:14*

Mr. Nettleton uses this verse to endorse his position on election on page 32 of his book. I would like to quote his statements concerning this under his heading of "Inability."

> *"...Neither can he know them..."* (1st Corinthians 2:14). Natural man, apart from God, is unable to comprehend spiritual truth. He is dead (Ephesians 2:1). It is necessary for the Holy Spirit of God to reprove (convince and convict) him (John 16:6-11)."

Let us examine the whole chapter of 1 Corinthians, Chapter 2, and we will find that Verse 14 is not referring to salvation whatsoever. All one has to do is to read the whole chapter and you will find out what the natural man is unable to comprehend about the things of God. It is not speaking about salvation, but is speaking about the things of the Christian that God has prepared for them after they are a Christian. Those are the things a lost man cannot comprehend. Proof of this is found in the second chapter of 1st Corinthians, beginning with Verse 9:

"But as it is written, Eye hath not seen, nor ear heard, neither have entered into the heart of man, the things which God hath prepared for them that love him."

In this portion of Scripture, God is speaking concerning the saved. As we go into Verse 10:

"But God hath revealed them unto us by his Spirit: for the Spirit searcheth all things, yea, the deep things of God."

Here God is speaking about the things that He has prepared for those that love Him; that is, after they are saved. Things that God has prepared, even the Rapture, this is hard for a lost man to comprehend.

For example. The Second Jerusalem, a city 1200 to 1500 miles square, containing the Tree of Life that bears 12 manner of fruit each season.

How the resurrected body of Christ could both eat and enjoy food and yet be a spiritual, resurrected body. How Christ's resurrected body could be seen, at times, and yet invisible, at other times, and yet that same body will never die.

Or, how God could create new heavens and a new earth. It is hard for a lost man to comprehend the Great White Throne Judgment, and the fact that all Christians will be there as spectators--

"so shall we ever be with the Lord." - 1 Thessalonians 4:17

It is hard for a lost man to comprehend all these things that God has prepared for the Christian. A lost man is unable to do that without the Holy Spirit. A lost man can believe on

94

the Lord Jesus Christ, because all through Paul's ministry he kept emphasizing the importance of using plainness of speech. In fact, he did this in 1 Corinthians 2:4,

"And my speech and my preaching was not with enticing words of man's wisdom, but in demonstration of the Spirit and of power:"

It was not *"with enticing words"* but words spoken in simplicity. A lost person *can understand* that Christ died in payment for their sin. A lost person can understand that God gives eternal life to anyone who will accept Christ as their Savior. No--God does not give you the faith to believe with, but rather gives His *Word* which we stand responsible for accepting or rejecting!

So--we see it would be out of context to use 1 Corinthians 2:14 as proof of "election for salvation."

"...the natural man cannot receive the things of the Spirit of God, they are foolishness unto him, neither can he know them (or understand them)."

All one has to do is go back to the other verses in this chapter and they will find out it is the <u>deep things</u> that God is speaking about and the things that God has prepared for those who love Him, after they are saved. It is hard for the lost to understand and believe such things until they trust Christ as Savior and they are indwelt with the Holy Spirit. The Holy Spirit enables a person to see the things God has prepared for him.

Notice in Verse 11:

"For what man knoweth the things of a man, save the spirit of man which is in him? even so the things of God knoweth no man, but the Spirit of God."

Notice the last part of Verse 11,

"...even so, the things of God knoweth no man, but the Spirit of God."

Notice the first part of Verse 12,

"Now we have received, not the spirit of the world."

The reason that we have not received the spirit of the world is that we possessed it from birth. We have received (the last part of Verse 12)

"...the spirit which is of God; that we might know the things that are freely given to us of God."

So, what the context is referring to is very simple. We cannot understand the things that God has promised to freely give the Christian after he is saved and the promises He has made to the Christian, until we first believe on the Lord Jesus Christ and are then indwelt with the Holy Spirit of God. In Verse 12 as it says,

"...that we might know the things that are freely given to us of God."

To say that 1 Corinthians 2:14 is inferring that a lost man cannot understand salvation, would be to eliminate the rest of the verses from the context and, also, violate a person's free will when God says "whosoever will may come."

The "election" proponents use this one verse and then reason that God will only convict by the Holy Spirit those whom He has elected to be saved; then only those will believe because God gives them the faith to do so. This can only be done when you take one verse and isolate the rest of the chapter. You see, the truth of the Word of God surfaces when the context of the whole chapter is examined.

In conclusion: After examining the context, Verse 14 speaks about the natural man receiving not the things of the Spirit of God. Why?

"...for they are foolishness unto him, neither can he know them because they are spiritually discerned." - 1 Corinthians 2:14b

The spiritual things that he cannot comprehend are revealed in Verses 9 through 12 and these things are what God has prepared for the Christian after he is saved. It is these things that the natural man is unable to comprehend without the Holy Spirit of God, not salvation!

24. Colossians 3:12 - Elect Because of Faith In Christ; Not, Elected For Salvation!

"Put on therefore, as the elect of God, holy and beloved, bowels of mercies, kindness, humbleness of mind, meekness, longsuffering." - Colossians 3:12

Mr. Nettleton has a habit of using little select quotes from verses in order to endorse his position of "election to salvation," without giving any context. One such instance is found on page 33 of his book and I should like to quote his comments.

"God addresses us as 'the elect of God. (Colossians 3:12)."

"Knowing, brethren beloved, your election of God."- (1 Thessalonians 1:4).

We are going to compare the whole verse of Colossians 3:12 and see if it agrees with the rest of the Scriptures given in the book of Colossians. Notice carefully, if you will, that Paul is addressing Christians at Colosse. He is speaking to those who have received Christ as Savior, as the elect, not that he is stating the mind of God to elect certain ones to be saved. Here, he is speaking to those who are *already* saved and instructing them as to what they ought to do since they are saved. This would totally agree with other Scriptures in Colossians.

For example. In Chapter 1, Verse 4, Paul stated in writing to the Colossians:

"Since we heard of your faith in Jesus Christ, and of the love which ye have to all the saints." - Colossians 1:4

There are two things to be observed: It was *their faith* in Christ Jesus (they had testified), then they had shown that faith *"which ye have to all saints."* Therefore, they had shown that *"which ye have."* God did not predestinate them to be saved. He did not predestinate them as far as serving Him, but it was their free choice. It is God's will but He did not make it come to pass. He left that free will for the Colossians to exercise. Again we would like to emphasize, *"Since we have heard of your faith in Christ Jesus, and of the love which ye have to all saints."*

For anyone to just extract *"the elect of God"* out of Colossians 3:12 without considering the rest of the verse; or the context, would be violating the very basic principles of biblical interpretation. We find out as we go on down to Verse 28 of Colossians, Chapter one:

"Whom we preach, warning every man, and teaching every man in all wisdom; that we may present every man prefect in Christ Jesus." - Colossians 1:28

It was evident that Paul did not believe in predestination-- as far as electing some to be saved and some to be lost. Because he said that "We...warn *every man*." So it is God's will that *every man* would be saved.

25. 1 Thessalonians 1:4 - "Elect" Based On Acceptance of Christ.

"Knowing, brethren beloved, your election of God."

Since Mr. Nettleton, on page 33 of his book, included 1 Thessalonians 1:4 along with Colossians 3:12, it is imperative that we examine the context and see the meaning of this verse. Nettleton accused some men who disagree with him on election as avoiding these two verses. His statement on page 33:

"By now it ought to be clearly recognized that God uses language that some men avoid."

The only thing we seek to avoid is doing what Mr. Nettleton did. That is, taking one little phrase or verse out of context without considering the rest of the chapter or other verses that relate to the same subject. Concerning Verse 4, you will find that God many times calls the saved "his elect" or "his chosen." But this is after the fact that they have put their faith in Jesus Christ. When a person accepts the Lord Jesus Christ as Savior, they are the chosen and referred to as the "chosen" or "the elect." Christians are referred to as "the elect" only on the basis of their acceptance of Christ.

Notice in Verses 7 and 8 where Paul states:

"So that ye were ensamples to all that believe in Macedonia and Achaia. (7) For from you sounded out the word of the Lord not only in Macedonia and Achaia, but also in every place your faith to Godward is spread abroad; so that we need not to speak anything." (8)

If you will notice that it says, *"but also in every place your faith."* It does not say "God's faith in you," but "your faith in Christ." You see, the Scriptures mean exactly what they say. I do not know how one could get "election to salvation" out of these verses when Paul speaks to them and says that it is "your faith that is spoken abroad." Not--"God's faith in you." It is "your faith in God" that you speak about so freely and strongly.

In fact, Paul said that he needed not to speak anything. There was not anything that Paul could add to what those in Thessalonica were doing. They were that strong in the faith and knew what they believed and were ready to stand behind it. Not because they were elected. They were only referred to as "God's elect" because they had put their faith in Christ out of their own volition and free will.

26. Revelation 7:4,5 - Sealed For Service; Not Chosen To Salvation!

"And I heard the number of them which were sealed: and there were sealed an hundred and forty and four thousand of all the tribes of the children of Israel. (4)

Of the tribe of Juda were sealed twelve thousand. Of the tribe of Reuben were sealed twelve thousand. Of the tribe of Gad were sealed twelve thousand." (5)

May I quote Mr. Nettleton's concluding statement after he used a portion of this Scripture to support election to salvation:

"If a person is saved, he was elected and no reason for that election is revealed to us."

There is no question that the author is applying these verses to election concerning salvation--not service, as his quote clarifies. The reason it is not revealed to us is because it is not true!

If one will only take time to examine Revelation, chapters 7 and 14, which are the only two chapters in the Bible that mention the 144,000, one will find that they are sealed for protection while serving Christ. The word "sealed" is the Greek verb "SPHRAGIZO" and means ownership and security, together with destination. In other words, they are saved Jews, protected from harm until their testimony for Christ is finished here on the earth.

"These are they which were not defiled with women; for they are virgins. These are they which follow the Lamb whithersoever he goeth. These were redeemed from among

men, being the firstfruits unto God and to the lamb." - Revelation 14:4

Calling the 144,000 the first fruits is in reference to their being some of the first ones saved at the beginning of the 7-year Tribulation. To say that God elected them to salvation is absolutely contrary to the Scriptures. My Bible says "sealed" for service; not "elected for salvation." In fact, the words "elect, election, or elected" do not appear anywhere in the book of Revelation! This is no doubt the greatest evangelistic campaign ever launched on the face of the earth by 144,000 saved, Jewish men.

Mr. Nettleton goes on to say:

"Dare we omit such doctrines when God teaches them? Surely, all Scripture is profitable (2 Timothy 3:16)."

In answer to this we say affirmatively, "No! We do not omit any Scripture, but we do not take a Scripture that is speaking about service and teach it as applying to salvation which only causes confusion to the reader. No--We do not insert our word "election" to replace God's word "sealed."

This is like taking the book of James and saying, "If you are not living the life, then you are not really saved." Some preachers try to use this as a scare tactic to attempt to scare people into living the Christian life. And yet, they have not reconciled the book of James with Romans which tells us we are saved by grace through faith. The book of Romans is justification in God's eyes by faith alone without works. And yet James says,

"If a man say he hath faith and has not works, his faith is dead."

Without recognizing that the book of James is justification in man's eyes, there is nothing but utter confusion in the believer's mind.

James is not saying that a person is lost without good works, only the fact that his faith is dead. It is lifeless unless he is living the kind of Christian life that will support his witness for Christ. In fact, there are a good many Christians who are not leading the Christian life, but it does not mean they are not saved.

One can arrive at any kind of doctrine they wish to endorse, by taking one verse and not correlating other Scriptures that shed light upon a particular subject. If one wills to know the truth of God's Word, then all Scripture on a certain subject must and will agree. Remember, the 144,000 spoken of in Revelation, chapters 7 and 14, is in reference to their service to Christ, not being elected by God to be saved. How simple God's Word is to understand if not infected by man's philosophy and self righteousness.

"False Doctrine Shipwrecks Souls"

"Foreknowledge, in Scripture, never determines what is to be--foreknowledge is only the knowledge of things to be beforehand. It is the same with our scientists, they can tell when there is to be an eclipse of the sun or of the moon: on a certain day at a certain hour, minute and second; but the scientists do not bring about the eclipse. God has foreknowledge, and by this foreknowledge knows the future, but that is where it ends."

Dr. Mark G. Cambron

"False Doctrine Shipwrecks Souls"

CHAPTER THREE

EXAMPLES OF THE FREE WILL OF MAN FOR SERVICE

1. Moses' Good Decision

> *"Choosing rather to suffer affliction with the people of God, than to enjoy the pleasures of sin for a season; (25)*
>
> *Esteeming the reproach of Christ greater riches than the treasures in Egypt: for he had respect unto the recompense of the reward. (26)*
>
> *By faith he forsook Egypt, not fearing the wrath of the king: for he endured, as seeing him who is invisible." - Hebrews 11:25 – 27*

Here we find Moses making a good choice out of his own free will. These verses state that Moses explicitly chose for himself as for a result of his own reasoning and analysis of the situation. He made his own decision to suffer affliction with God's people, Israel, rather than to enjoy the pleasures of sin for a season. It was Moses' responsibility and decision to do that. We also stand responsible for our decisions.

2. Moses' Bad Decision

"For he supposed his brethren would have understood how that God by his (Moses') hand would deliver them (Israel): but they understood not."- Acts 7:25

God had called Moses to deliver the nation of Israel out of bondage from the nation of Egypt after 400+ years. The circumstances relating to Moses' disobedience of that calling and his spending 40 years on the back side of the desert in wasted time is recorded in Exodus 2 and 3. Now, notice Acts 7:29-30:

"Then fled Moses at this saying, and was a stranger in the land of Midian, where he begat two sons. And when <u>forty years</u> were expired, there appeared to him in the wilderness of Mount Sina an angel of the Lord in a flame of fire in a bush."

You see Moses wasted 40 years by willfully disobeying God's will for him to lead the children of Israel out of bondage. After 40 years on the back side of the desert, Exodus 3 reveals to us that the Angel of the Lord appeared unto Moses in a flame of fire out of the midst of a bush. After dealing with Moses in this manner, Exodus 3:10 enlightens us that God again seeks to have Moses obey His will as He commands him again to go unto Pharaoh. My question is, "Would God ask Moses to lead the children of Israel and then put it into Moses' mind to be disobedient to God's command?" This would be unbelievable! We do find, though, that Moses out of his own free will chose to disobey God. God did not over-ride the free will of Moses. Forty years later God dealt with Moses again and this time Moses chose to obey.

3.   Moses' Choice To Take Advice.

> *"So Moses hearkened to the voice of his father-in-law, and did all that he had said." - Exodus 18:24*

In reading all of Exodus 18, we find that *Moses made a choice* to choose able men to help him in judging the nation of Israel, based in the advice of his father-in-law. You will recall that Jethro, Moses' father-in-law, had witnessed Moses judging all the people by himself which became a tremendous burden. Notice in Verse 14:

> *"And when Moses' father-in-law saw all that he did to the people, he said, What is this thing that thou doest to the people? Why sittest thou thyself alone, and all the people stand by thee from morning unto even?"*

What Moses was doing took up all of his time. We are told in Verse 18:

> *"Thou wilt surely wear away, both thou, and this people that is with thee: for this thing is too heavy for thee; thou art not able to perform it thyself alone."*

We find that the advice of Moses' father-in-law was to search out people, teach them and allow them to help Moses in the work. We find this in Verse 21:

> *"Moreover thou shalt provide out of all the people able men, such as fear God, men of truth, hating covetousness; and place such over them, to be rulers of thousands, and rulers of hundreds, rulers of fifties, and rulers of tens."*

Moses' response is recorded in Verse 24:

> *"So Moses hearkened to the voice of his father-in-law, and did all that he had said."*

Moses chose able men from all Israel and made them heads over the people. Notice Moses' reasoning for whom he chose in Verse 25:

> *"They were able men."*

God chooses us on the basis of our faith in the Lord Jesus Christ. The point is, Moses had a right to make a choice. Here he took the advice of his father-in-law, which was very good advice. But again, Moses had the free will in order to make a choice or reject the advice of Jethro. God uses people to take the Gospel and influence others to put their faith in Christ. In Romans 10:17 we are told that:

> *"...faith cometh by hearing, and hearing by the word of God."*

God uses Christians to help other Christians. We, as Christians, should listen to other Christians and at least hear what they have to say. We can benefit from their experience and knowledge and then make our decisions based on the Word of God. A wise pastor will always listen to the advice of experienced deacons, as many times they have good sound advice. They can be a tremendous help to a pastor with their experience. Therefore, each one of us is responsible for the decisions that we make. God never imposes His will to override our free will to make those decisions.

4. Lot's Choices.

> *"Then Lot chose him all the plain of Jordan; and Lot journeyed east: and they separated themselves the one from the other." - Genesis 13:11*

As one studies the Biblical record we find that Lot continually made the wrong choice. Would one dare to accuse God of electing Lot to do the wrong things, to choose sin, and be disobedient? If you read the story as recorded in the entire 13th chapter, you find there was a strife between the herdsmen of Abraham and those of Lot. Abraham had the right attitude as revealed in Verses 8 and 9:

> *"And Abraham said unto Lot, let there be no strife, I pray thee, between me and thee, and between my herdmen and thy herdmen; for we be brethren. (8) Is not the whole*

land before thee? separate thyself, I pray thee, from me; if thou wilt take the left hand, then I will go to the right; or if thou depart to the right hand, then I will go to the left." (9)

Again, in Verse 11, we find that, "Lot chose." It was his decision. One can hardly say that God made Lot make the wrong choice, or you would have God making a wrong decision. No, Lot was not elected to do that. Here you find the free will of Lot to make his own choice. Notice in Verse 10:

"And Lot lifted up his eyes, and beheld all the plain of Jordan, that it was well watered everywhere, before the Lord destroyed Sodom and Gomorrah, even as the garden of the LORD, like the land of Egypt, as thou comest unto Zoar."

Lot's choice was made by sight, not by faith. Notice, again, if you will in Verse 12:

"Abram dwelled in the land of Canaan, and Lot dwelled in the cities of the plain, and pitched his tent towards Sodom."

This was Lot's second wrong choice. The next wrong decision Lot made is recorded in Genesis 14:12:

*"And they took Lot, Abram's brother's son, **who dwelt in Sodom,** and his goods, and departed."*

Here we find out that *Lot* *has* *chosen* to live in Sodom. That surely was not God's will, but Lot made *his own choice*. Again Lot made his own choice, as he sat in the gate of Sodom, as recorded in Genesis 19:1:

*"And there came two angels to Sodom at even; and **Lot sat in the gate of Sodom:** and Lot seeing them rose up to meet them; and he bowed himself with his face toward the ground."*

Now he is sitting in the gate of Sodom. This may reveal that he held a position of some importance in this wicked city! Yet it was not God's will that he do this. But God permitted Lot to make his own choice. Lot was then visited by two angels from God as we have recorded in Genesis 19:4:

> *"But before they lay down, the men of the city, even the men of Sodom, compassed the house round, both old and young, all the people from every quarter."*

These were homosexuals. The name of the city of Sodom is where we get our word "sodomy."

Now Verse 5:

> *"And they called unto Lot, and said unto him, Where are the men which came in unto thee this night? Bring them out unto us, that we may <u>know</u> them."*

It is not talking about meeting them and shaking hands-- rather it is speaking about knowing them intimately! What a mess it was in Sodom! In Verse 7 we find Lot's unbelievable response. Would one dare to accuse God of choosing Lot to do this? Then, you would have God electing Lot to sin. Notice the record in Verse 7:

> *"And said, I pray you, brethren, do not so wickedly."*

There would not be anything wicked about shaking hands with them, but to know them as far as having a sexual relationship (homosexuality), of course, it was wicked! Notice what Lot decided to do in Verse 8:

> *"Behold now, I have two daughters which have not known man; let me, I pray you, bring them out unto you, and do ye to them as is good in your eyes: only unto these men do nothing: for therefore came they under the shadow of my roof."*

We cannot blame God for Lot's choice. We must charge Lot with a bad decision made of his own free will. Therefore, God is righteous in judging Lot. If God's election over-ruled the free will of man, then Lot would be justified in accusing God of electing him to prostitute his daughters. How ridiculous! If God's election over-rides the free will of man, then Lot would not have made the decision that he made.

If one is going to use the words "election" and "choosing" as far as the positive sense, then the only thing left is the negative! If you have two cars and elect to drive one, the other is left. If you elect to drive the other, then the opposite is left. If you elect someone to serve you, then you find out that he has no choice but to serve you.

Did God elect Lot to do this evil that he did? Absolutely not! God did not elect him and then control his mind to offer his two daughters to the perverted immorality of the homosexuals. Again the Scriptures reveal to us that Lot is a prime example of man's free will as he must stand responsible for his decisions.

We find that Lot lost everything because he made the wrong choices. He was saved, yet so as by fire. In fact, we would never know that Lot was ever saved if it were not for the New Testament writings of Peter in 2 Peter 2:6,7:

> *"And turning the cities of Sodom and Gomorrah into ashes condemned them with an overthrow, making them an example unto those that after should live ungodly; (6) And delivered just Lot, vexed with the filthy conversation of the wicked." (7)*

No one would ever have known Lot was saved as he continually made one wrong decision after another. Lot paid the price for his sinning and stood responsible for the choices he made. He *lifted up his eyes toward Sodom*, he had *moved toward Sodom*, he had *dwelt in Sodom*, and then *sat in the gate at Sodom*. Then Lot says in Verse 14:

> *"...for the Lord will destroy this city."*

Yes, God would not destroy the city until Lot came out. But Lot lost his wife, his home, and his possessions. God gave Lot a free will to make his own decisions, which he did, but he had to stand responsible for them.

In like manner, God tells us in Romans 14:10:

*"But why dost thou judge thy brother? or why dost thou set at nought thy brother? for we shall all stand before the judgment seat of Christ. For it is written, As I live, saith the Lord, **every knee shall bow to me**, and every tongue shall confess to God."*

Now in Verse 12:

*"So then **every one** of us shall give account of himself to God."*

How can we give account of ourselves to God if we are already elected and predestinated to do certain things? Then why give an account to God, if we would automatically do them? There would be nothing to account for. We would be like robots who have been programmed, having no choice of our own. Therefore, we would just be a machine on which God pushes a button and we automatically do it. What do we have to give an account for? It would be impossible to refuse God's will, even if we wanted to. No, we have a free will so we shall <u>all</u> give account of ourselves unto God. We are held responsible, as we have a free will in choosing to serve Christ or disobey Him with our lives.

5.   The Judgment Seat of Christ.

"For we must all appear before the judgment seat of Christ: that every one may receive the things done in his body, according to that he hath done, whether it be good or bad." - 2 Corinthians 5:10

Those who endorse "election" must realize that if it is impossible for a Christian to resist God's electing or choosing for service, then that Christian must have his old nature eradicated when he was saved. Rather, this verse reveals to us

112

that we are responsible for our actions. We are going to be judged at the judgment Seat of Christ for our rewards or loss of rewards according to what we have done. It is our choice. In other words, if we were programmed to serve Christ with no choice or free will, then why be judged for something we are not responsible for?

We find in our criminal courts today that a person judged mentally incompetent is not held responsible for what they do. The court would not judge a person guilty or not guilty if one is incapable of being responsible. If we were elected to serve Christ with no free will, then we would make no decision that is contrary to God's will. We would never get in a backslidden condition. The doctrine of election attacks the Word of God from every angle. It is never complimentary to God's Word nor does it agree with God's Word. Remember, *"we must __ALL__ appear before the Judgment Seat of Christ."* You see, we stand responsible for the decisions that God allows us to make with our free will.

6. Israel's Idolatry.

"Then said I unto them, Cast ye away every man the abominations of his eyes, and defile not yourselves with the idols of Egypt: I am the Lord your God. (7)

But they rebelled against me, and would not hearken unto me: they did not every man cast away the abominations of their eyes, neither did they forsake the idols of Egypt : then I said, I will pour out my fury upon them, to accomplish my anger against them in the midst of the land of Egypt." - Ezekiel 20:7,8

It would be preposterous to say that God directed their minds so they would not put away their idols after He had already commanded them to do so. One would have to conclude this, if God elected them and imposed His will over

113

their free will. We know it was God's will, even before creation, that all the Christians *"should be without blame and Holy before Him in love"* (Ephesians 1:4). Ezekiel 20:7,8 reveals God's will--as God commanded them to put away their idols. They could have only rebelled against the Lord if they possessed a free will, which they did.

7. David's Adultery.

In 1 Kings 8:16b we find that God had chosen David to be king over the nation of Israel:

> *"...but I chose David to be over my people of Israel."*

This was God's choice for David. Let me ask this question, "Did God make David accept the kingship over the nation of Israel? No, that was David's choice to accept or reject. Was it God's choice for David to commit adultery with Bathsheba? Absolutely not! God judged that sin by taking their first son by death (2 Samuel 12:14).

You see, it was God's choice for David to be king over Israel, but David could have rejected God's will. It was not God's will for David to commit adultery and first degree murder, but David went against the will of God in committing these acts. In this we see the free will of David, which God extends to everyone. David went against the will of God at one time and fulfilled the will of God at another.

In like manner the New Testament in Ephesians 4:11,12 reveals God's will:

> *"And he gave some, apostles, and some prophets; and some, evangelists; and some, pastors and teachers; For the perfecting of the saints, for the work of the ministry, for the edifying of the body of Christ."*

We can see that God has called some to be pastors, evangelists, and some to be teachers. He has called all Christians to edify the body of Christ; some with their voices, some with instruments, but all with the talents and abilities that God has given them. The sad part about it is--that some Christians are not utilizing their abilities for Christ. God will not make us do the service wherein He has called us. We must submit out of our own free will.

I know pastors who have been called into the ministry and after being in the pastorate awhile, become discouraged. Now they are no longer in the pastorate. Are the gifts of God without repentance? No!

> "For the gifts and calling of God are without repentance." - Romans 11:29

No, God has not forsaken or changed His mind about our calling. If we have forsaken the calling of the Lord, is God responsible? No!

The point we are making is, if God elected them to do that service and they possessed no free will, then they would still be in the pastorate as they would never have a desire to quit. Their free will would have been eradicated when they became saved and they would just go ahead and gladly do the will of God. You see, if election means God over-rides our free will, then no one would ever get out of the will of God. It is sad today as we see many Christians making the wrong decisions out of their free will.

> "And how shall they preach, except they be sent? as it is written, How beautiful are the feet of them that preach the gospel of peace, and bring glad tidings of good things!" - Romans 10:15

How is this accomplished? By doing so out of their own free will, motivated by love.

8. Free Will Concerning Marriage and Divorce

> "It hath been said, _whosoever_ shall put away his wife, let him give her a writing of divorcement: (31) But I say unto

you, that <u>whosoever</u> shall put away his wife, saving for the cause of fornication, causeth her to commit adultery: and <u>whosoever</u> shall marry her that is divorced committeth adultery."- Matthew 5:31,32

Notice that God says *"whosoever."* It is <u>never</u> God's will for two Christians to seek a divorce. It is sad today that many Christians are getting divorced. This is totally unnecessary and against God's will, but is the result of one or both persons getting out of fellowship with the Lord. Even though it is not God's will, it still happens many, many times.

I have a lot of friends, even some that were in Bible college, that are now divorced and yet they are saved people. Years ago I attended a meeting and listened to a great evangelist. This man has since been divorced and is now in the pastorate at a small church in one of the southern states. This was not God's will--no matter what the reasons are--but, nevertheless, the divorce was obtained out of their own will, which was contrary to God's will.

God does reveal His will in His Word, the Bible, but He does not, in His sovereignty, over-ride the free will of man. If that were not true, then there would never be a divorce and God would have controlled all the actions of the men in His service. Rather, we find the free will of man making decisions sometimes contrary to the will of God.

9.   Free Will Concerning Our Testimony

"<u>Whosoever</u> therefore shall confess me before men, him will I confess also before my Father which is in heaven. (32) But <u>whosoever</u> shall deny me before men, him will I also deny before my Father which is in heaven." - Matthew 10:32,33

If we begin with the first part of Chapter 10, we find that the disciples were told to go out as Christ had chosen them and given them their instructions.

He states in Verse 22:

"And ye shall be hated of all men for my name's sake, but he that endureth to the end shall be saved."

Therefore, if they endured to the end of their ministry they would be saved alive. We find that they were protected until God was through with their ministry. In Verse 30:

"But the very hairs of your head are all numbered."

Now we come on down to Verses 32 and 33:

"Whosoever therefore shall confess me before men, him will I confess also before my Father which is in heaven, (32) But whosoever shall deny me before men, him will I also deny before my Father which is in heaven." (33)

Here, again, we find that they had a free choice. Christ goes on to tell them in Verses 35 and 40 that they are going to have trouble with their own households. But they have a choice. Will they yield to some of their relatives? He also tells them in Verse 36:

"And a man's foes shall be they of his own household."

In other words, if you love your father and mother more than me, then you are not worthy to be my disciple. So, they had a choice to make. Many today have the same problem and the same instructions apply.

There are many that are out of the ministry because the wife would not let go of her mother and father. Or the husband would not let go of his mother and father. I remember one Catholic man I led to the Lord and later performed his wedding. His parents were staunch Roman Catholics and did everything imaginable to break up his marriage and get him out of our church. It came to the point where he finally had to tell them, "Don't come to my home anymore and I will not be back to see you because I am getting tired of you trying to take away from me what I have in Jesus Christ!" You see--he had a choice. He could have yielded to the influence and listened to his mother and father. But he did not--the choice was his. The conviction of the Holy Spirit will always be at work. But it never impedes over the free will of man.

Notice in Verse 32:

"...if you will confess me."

And in Verse 33:

"...if you deny me."

You see--the choice is ours. We can be a witness for Christ or we can deny Christ before men. Christ assures them that He will confess to the Father their faithfulness or unfaithfulness and they will be judged by their decision. We stand responsible for the decisions we make.

10. Your Free Will To Use Your Life For Christ

"For whosoever will save his life shall lose it: and whosoever will lose his life for my sake shall find it." - Matthew 16:25

Notice the "whosoever." It is your choice. These verses in context are speaking about our service to Christ, as we have a choice. If you save your life for yourself, then you will lose--or forfeit--what rewards you could have had in Christ by using your life for Him. And then He goes on to say:

"And 'whosoever' shall lose his life for my sake, shall find it."

When your life is hid in Christ, you will find out what living is really all about. This is when you put the Lord Jesus Christ first in your life. The point we are making is-- "whosoever" is your choice. If you save your life for yourself, you are going to reap the results. If you allow your life to be used for Christ, then you will also reap the rewards in Heaven as well as a satisfying life down here.

If man has no free will, then why did Christ give two alternatives? We thank God for giving us a free will. The Lord wants us to serve Him out of love, "because He first loved us," not because we are robots with no will of our own.

11. A Right Attitude.

"And <u>whosoever</u> shall exalt himself shall be abased; and he that shall humble himself shall be exalted." -Matthew 23:12

Again we are told that we have the right to make our own choice. Here centers one of the main problems in churches as well as individual lives today. Sometimes you will find in a church someone trying to "play the role" of pastor or occupy the position "ex officio." They are the church's "bully" and seem to want everyone to look upon them as the "big cheese" of the church. These are they who are filled with pride. They are the "Diotrephes" of the church - 3 John 9,10.

God says that He will exalt those who humble themselves. God loves a humble person. The person who many times will avoid an argument. That person is not trying to "show off" in the church, but realizes they are <u>what</u> they are by the grace of God.

Notice--the choice is ours. "<u>Whosoever</u>" will humble himself, God will exalt. Christians do have a choice as to how they are going to act concerning their pride. "Whosoever" tells us that we have the right to make that choice ourselves. Allow me to ask you what is your attitude toward your position in the church? What is your attitude toward your pastor, toward other people and toward yourself? Have you tried to exalt yourself? Have you humbled yourself, realizing you are what you are by the grace of God?

119

I would not want to be a machine with God controlling my mind so that I would not have a free will to use as God created it. It is very clear that we stand responsible for our own actions and behavior, whether we exalt ourselves or humble ourselves in the sight of God.

12. Our Christian Walk.

"But whoso keepeth his word, in him verily is the love of God perfected: hereby know we that we are in him." - 1 John 2:5

This is speaking about how a Christian should act. Now Verse 6:

"He that saith he abideth in him ought himself also so to walk, even as he walked."

As a Christian, we can say one thing and do another-- depending upon what kind of life *we choose* to live. *"Whoso keepeth His word."* The "whoso" here is your choice! We have a right to keep His word, and if we do, God says:

"...In him verily is the love of God perfected. Hereby know we that we are in him."

When we have that kind of fellowship, walking that kind of life, it is tremendous to have that assurance that it is being accomplished by our yielding to the conviction of the Holy Spirit, as directed by the Word of God. The choice is ours!

Notice again in Verse 6:

"He that saith he abideth in him ought himself also so to walk, even as he walked."

The word *"ought"* shows obligation, indebtedness, duty and the free will to obey or disobey God's will. Contrast the word *"ought"* here with the word *"shall"* in Romans 14:10-12, where Christians *"shall"* (with no choice) give account of themselves at the Judgment Seat of Christ. For the doctrine of election to be true, God should have used the word "shall" instead of "ought" in 1 John 2:6. Either God is confused or those who endorse the doctrine of election are--the choice is yours.

13. Obedience.

> *"Whosoever committeth sin transgresseth also the law: for sin is the transgression of the law." - 1 John 3:4*

Notice, again, that it is our choice. We are grateful for those "whosoever's" that serve the Lord! But there are also the "whosoever's" who do not serve the Lord. Nevertheless, the right of choice is extended to each and every person. We thank God for those who have chosen to yield their bodies as a living sacrifice to God. Those that are serving. But they are doing so out of their own free will that God has given them.

In Verse 6 we have the same thing:

> *"Whosoever abideth in Him sinneth not: whosoever sinneth hath not seen Him, neither know Him."*

Notice the choice. *"Whosoever abideth in him."* If you abide in Him, you are not sinning when you are yielding yourself a living sacrifice unto God, which is our reasonable service (Romans 12:1,2). It is God's will that we live that kind of Christian life, but not always does the Christian yield to God's will. God never imposes His will by taking away the free will that He has graciously given to every person. As we said, God desires His Children to serve Him out of love *"because He first loved us."*

14. The Lord's Supper

> *"Wherefore whosoever shall eat this bread, and drink this cup of the Lord, unworthily, shall be guilty of the body and blood of the Lord." - 1 Corinthians 11:27*

Here we find the Lord extends to the Christian the choice of examining himself. Again, notice the <u>whosoever</u> in this verse. Then in Verse 28:

"But let a man <u>examine himself</u>..."

God gives the right to every Christian to determine what condition they are in and what their motives are for partaking of the Lord's Supper. The decision is ours. God had instructed the Apostle Paul through the Holy Spirit to write and instruct those at Corinth concerning the reason that judgment had been brought upon some of these Christians. The record is found in Verses 29 and 32:

"For he that eateth and drinketh unworthily, eateth and drinketh damnation to himself, not discerning the Lord's body." (29)

The word "damnation" is the Greek word "krima" and it means "judgment" not "damnation to Hell." In other words, when they partook of the Lord's Supper unworthily they drank to themselves judgment. Verse 30 explains the judgment that was rendered:

"For this cause many are weak and sickly among you, and many sleep."

In other words, many have died. This was the Lord's chastening for the way they had partaken of the Lord's Supper. The admonition is given in Verses 31 and 32:

"For if we would judge ourselves, we should not be judged. (31) But when we are judged, we are chastened of the Lord, that we should not be condemned with the world." (32)

One of the reasons that initiated this chastening was their preparation of a "love feast" prior to the Lord's Supper. They would call together all the dignitaries and the "big shots" and actually get themselves drunk! They would stuff themselves with food, use the vomitoriums, then re-eat, making a mockery out of the Lord's Supper. This is made clear from 1 Corinthians 11:20-22:

"When ye come together therefore into one place, this is not to eat the Lord's Supper. (20)

For in eating every one taketh before his own supper: and one is hungry, and another is drunken. (21)

What? have ye not houses to eat and to drink in? or despise ye the church of God, and shame them that have not? What shall I say to you? shall I praise you in this? I praise you not." (22)

Then God tells them to judge in themselves to eliminate God's judgment and chastening. Again, the reason many of them died and were sick, physically, was because of God's chastening.

Notice man's free will in these verses. Verse 31:

"...if we would judge ourselves."

Then in Verse 28:

"...let a man examine himself,"

Also in Verse 27:

"Whosoever shall eat of this bread and drink of this cup of the Lord unworthily."

The choice is entirely left to the individual Christian as to how and in what manner he partakes of the Lord's Supper. Each Christian is held responsible for their actions by the Lord. The Holy Spirit within us will always convict us to do the right thing. It is the Spirit that convicts of sin, righteousness and judgment and the Holy Spirit always seeks for us to yield to the will of God. It is God's will but our choice whether we use our mind and lives for Jesus Christ, that we may be found "unto the praise of His glory at his returning." If election to service is true, then how could these Christians resist God's will in doing what they did?

123

15. Civil Obedience.

> "Let every soul be subject unto the higher powers. For there is no power but of God: the powers that be are ordained of God. (1)
>
> Whosoever therefore resisteth the power, resisteth the ordinance of God: and they that resist shall receive to themselves damnation." - Romans 13:1,2

The Lord goes on to instruct us in Verse 4 that the judge is:

> "...a minister of God to thee for good."

Notice that the Lord extends the choice to us in Verse 2:

> "Whosoever therefore resisteth the power..."

Those who do resist the power are actually resisting God, because these powers are ordained of God. The "whosoever" tells us that God does not impose His will over the free will of the Christian. Do you know any Christian who has not broken some law of the land? Of course, you do not. If election were true, then no Christian would ever break any law or do anything wrong because they would be unable to resist the will of God. It is God's will that we obey the civil laws of our land as a testimony for Him, but God never makes us do that. You see, God rewards the Christian for his obedience.

If a Christian did not have a free will, then God would be rewarding Himself.

16. Pouting Elijah.

> "But he himself went a day's journey into the wilderness, and came and sat down under a juniper tree: and he requested for himself that he might die; and said, it is enough; now, O LORD, take away my life; for I am not better than my fathers." - 1 Kings 19:4

124

You may recall the story concerning Elijah--how that God had chosen him to be His servant. At one point in Elijah's life, he felt sorry for himself and chose rather to pout under the juniper tree, instead of going ahead and serving the Lord. God had to deal with him concerning this. There are times in every one of our lives when God may be directing us to do a certain task, but we fail to respond immediately. We must recognize and admit that not every Christian is obedient to the will of God. The reason--we have a free choice. The cause of disobedience is the old nature. The point is, Elijah reacted against God because of his own free will. Did God direct Elijah to ask Him to take his life? Of course not!

Notice in Romans 12:1, 2:

"I beseech (beg) you therefore, brethren, by the mercies of God, that ye present your bodies a living sacrifice, holy, acceptable unto God, which is your reasonable service. (1) And be not conformed to this world: but be ye transformed by the renewing of your mind, that ye may prove what is that good, and acceptable, and perfect, will of God." (2)

Why have these verses in the Bible if the Christian has no free will to disobey?

17. Peter's Denial

"And Peter remembered the word of Jesus, which said unto him, Before the cock crow, thou shalt deny me thrice. And he went out, and wept bitterly." - Matthew 26:75

It was not God's will that Peter deny Christ three times. It is not God's will that any of us should deny Christ. Peter's three denials of Christ are recorded in Matthew 26:69-75. You see, Peter possessed a free will to confess Christ or to deny Him. Allow me to ask you, as a Christian, have you ever denied Christ by failing to witness to someone when the opportunity was there?

125

Later on, our Lord gave Peter an opportunity to confess Him three times. The record is found in John 21:15-17. At one time Peter chose to deny Christ, later on Peter chose to confess Christ. Peter possessed a free will, just as you and I. Notice in Romans 6:16:

> "Know ye not, that to whom ye yield yourselves servants to obey, his servants ye are to whom ye obey; whether of sin unto death, or of obedience unto righteousness?"

We, as Christians, can be spiritually alive or spiritually dead, depending upon whom _we yield ourselves to._

18. Daniel's Decision Not To Be Defiled

> "But Daniel purposed in his heart that he would not defile himself with the portion of the king's meat, nor with the wine which he drank: therefore he requested of the prince of the eunuchs that he might not defile himself." - Daniel 1:8

You see, Daniel made his own decision that he would not be defiled by the meat from the king's table. God did not elect him to do that or choose him to do that with no free will of his own. Of course, it was God's will that he live a separated life, but again, God did not over-ride Daniel's right to make that decision for himself.

19. Contentious Christians.

> "For it hath been declared unto me of you, my brethren, by them which are of the house of Chloe, that there are contentions among you. (11) Now this I say, that every one of you saith, I am of Paul; and I of Apollos; and I of Cephas; and I of Christ."- 1 Corinthians 1:11,12

Was it God's will that there were contentions among the Christians, as they were choosing up sides and following different men? The answer is--No, that was not God's will. If election means they will always do God's will, then they would not have done this out of their own free will.

As one would study the whole book of 1st Corinthians, we find out the various things that these Christians were doing were very, very "un-Christian-like" in conduct. They were the most carnal church in all the world at that time. However, it was not God's will that they remain carnal. It was God's will that they grow up to be spiritual Christians, not little babies in Christ. This is what Paul spoke about in chapter 3, Verse 1:

> *"And I, brethren, could not speak unto you as unto spiritual, but as unto carnal, even as unto babes in Christ."*

How could those at Corinth be unspiritual if it was God's will that they be spiritual, if they had no free will of their own? In 1st Corinthians 1:2 we find that these Christians were...

> *"...sanctified in Christ Jesus..."*

...yet they had not grown enough to live a practical sanctification or separation unto God. The free will of man stands out as God did not withdraw their right of decision. He will deal with us in chastening because He loves us too much to allow us to continue in disobedience. The choice is ours and we will stand responsible!

20. Jeremiah's Choice.

> *"Then the word of the Lord came unto me, saying, Before I formed thee in the belly I knew thee; and before thou camest forth out of the womb I sanctified thee, and I ordained thee a prophet unto the nations." - Jeremiah 1:4,5*

God said that He knew Jeremiah while he was yet in his mother's womb, and that He had chosen him for service. This is God's will for the prophet, Jeremiah, and it does reveal the will of God. It is true that God revealed His will for Jeremiah before he was ever born. It now becomes Jeremiah's choice whether he will yield to God's will or not (Read all of Psalms 139, especially noticing Verses 13 and 16 concerning God's omniscience about every individual before they are born). Jeremiah, like many of us, tried to excuse himself from God's calling. Notice in Jeremiah 1:6:

> *"Then said I, Ah, Lord GOD! behold, I cannot speak: for I am a child."*

If election to service were true, then Jeremiah would have automatically been jubilant and excited over hearing about God's will for him. But such was not the case at first. Many Christians, like Jeremiah, change their mind and go on to serve the Lord. But we also find that many do not, which is sad and tragic! As His children, God wants <u>ALL</u> of us to serve Him. If election were true, over-riding the free will of man, then all Christians would automatically want to serve Christ and there would never be any need for chastening!

21. A Personal Friend.

While in Bible college and in my Senior year, a good friend of mine possessed "straight A's" in school. When the day of our final exams arrived, my friend did not show up. He left school and did not take his final exams; therefore, he did not graduate. Was this God's will for him? Absolutely not! God wanted him to finish the course, as Paul has stated in Acts 20:24:

> *"But none of these things move me, neither count I my life dear unto myself, so that I might finish my course with joy, and the ministry, which I have received of the Lord Jesus, to testify the gospel of the grace of God."*

The glorious part about this story is that my friend came back to school some time later, completing his final exams and graduated from college. He is now a missionary in Argentina, doing a great work for the Lord. Was that God's will that he dropped out of school? I think not! Did God direct him to drop out? Absolutely not! Being close to my friend while going through college, I was aware of the circumstances that brought this about. God allowed him to make his choice; then, later, to reconsider and finish the calling God had for him.

We do thank God for His patience with us as He directs us by His Word and conviction of the Holy Spirit--always allowing us our free will to serve Him. God wants you to serve Him out of love--not because we are some machine with no free will at all. My friend was responsible for the decisions he made. I am grateful he finally made the right decision to finish the course and answer by yielding to the calling of God.

22. Pastor Younce

When I first trusted Christ as Savior, I knew that I was doing things God did not want me to do. Drinking and other things were not God's will for my life after I was saved, but for a year I still did a lot of those things. I knew that I was saved and that I still possessed eternal life because it was not predicated upon my good works. When I was saved, God never rescinded my free will. It was God's will and through the conviction of the Holy Spirit and influence of other Christians, my life began to change. Later, I dedicated my life to Christ and went ahead and followed the leading of the Lord, going to Bible college and getting prepared for the ministry.

One must remember, this was God's will; but, it was my choice. God did not make me do it. I could have resisted If I had wanted to, and at times there was much opposition against fulfilling God's will for my life. I had difficult decisions to make but I chose to go ahead and put the Lord first in that respect. But I did not have to. Again, God did not take away my free will or my right to make that choice. God did His part, as far as convicting and leading, but it was then up to me to decide if I would yield to God's will or reject it.

Should I seek to please men and stay on the job I had with security, or seek to please the Lord and quit that job to enter Bible school? Again, I thank God that He did not make me a robot but allowed me to choose to serve Him out of love. My free will was not over-ridden by the Lord. I was allowed to make that choice and I thank God for that. You and I must stand responsible for the decisions we make because of the free will that God has given us.

23. Israel

"Brethren, my heart's desire and prayer to God for Israel is, that they might be saved." - Romans 10:1

Paul's will corresponded with God's will that all Israel be saved. This corresponds with many other portions of the Word of God where He is *"not willing any should perish but that all should come to repentance."* If election to salvation were true, then every Jewish person would be saved because they would have no free will to reject God's call by the Gospel. Yet, we find that not all Israel is saved. Each individual Jewish person has a free will to receive or reject Christ. If election were true, then no Jewish person would ever be lost. Here, again, surfaces the free will of man.

24. "All" Means "All!"

"All we like sheep have gone astray; we have turned every one to his own way; and the Lord hath laid on him the iniquity of us all." - Isaiah 53:6

If the Satanic doctrine of election to salvation is true, then we would have to conclude that this verse is an outright

130

lie! This verse explicitly declares two facts: One is that we have <u>all</u> sinned and gone astray, the second is that God has allowed Christ to pay for the sins of <u>everyone</u>.

One man has rightly said, "If we want to know how to be saved as it includes everyone, you go in at the first <u>all</u> and come out at the last <u>all</u>, and you have been saved."

You see, no one is excluded. All the sheep have gone astray; therefore, God Laid upon Christ the iniquity of us all. Why would Christ pay the penalty for the sins of all if <u>all</u> could not be saved? There is no basis for God to choose or reject anyone other than their acceptance or rejection of Christ.

God's character never changes. God is Holy, God is Righteous and God loves the whole world--even while we were sinners. Notice in Romans 5:8...

> *"But God commendeth his love toward us, in that, while we were sinners, Christ died for us."*

The Lord's will is for <u>all</u> to be saved as we are <u>all</u> sinners. Revelation 22:17 limits no one :

> *"And <u>whosoever</u> <u>will</u>, let him take of the water of life freely."*

25. Christ Is The Light.

> *"In him was life; and the life was the light of men." (4)*
> *"That was the true Light, which lighteth <u>every man</u> that cometh into the world." (9) - John 1:4,9*

The doctrine of election is contrary to God's will as seen in these verses. The light of the Lord Jesus Christ <u>lights</u> <u>every man</u> that is born into the world. Notice in Verse 7:

> *"The same come for a witness, to bear witness of the light, that <u>all</u> <u>men</u> through him might believe.*

"All men." This is God's will. Every man born possesses the illumination that there is a Divine Creator. This

131

corresponds perfectly with other portions of the Word of God such as Romans 1:19,20:

> *"Because that which may be known of God is manifest in them; for God hath shewed it unto them. (19)*
>
> *For the invisible things of him from the creation of the world are clearly seen, being understood by the things that are made, even his eternal power and Godhead; so that they are without excuse." (20)*

Man has a God-given sense when he is born to know there is a Creator, so that no man can claim an excuse. Verse 20 tells us that man has the knowledge of a Divine Creator by the things he can see--the stars, the sky, the moon, and the things that no man could create or set in order. This is attested to also by Isaiah 45:6...

> *"That they may know from the rising of the sun, and from the west, that there is none beside me. I am the LORD, and there is none else."*

Why would God instill this knowledge in <u>everyone</u> if it was not God's will for <u>everyone</u> to acknowledge Him, and be saved?

A.   Those Who Have A Desire To Know Christ.

An example of this was a man by the name of Cornelius. We find his story recorded in Acts 10. Cornelius was a man who had a desire to know God but did not know Christ. He was a lost man, yet he had a desire to know the Creator. No one had told him about the Lord Jesus Christ. Where did he get the knowledge that there was a God? Acts 10:1 tells us that:

> *"There was a certain man in Caesarea called Cornelius, a centurion of the band called the Italian band. He was a devout man, and one that <u>feared</u> God with all of his house,*

132

which gave much alms to the people, and prayed to God alway."

If you were a neighbor to Cornelius at that time, you would have concluded that he was saved, but he was not. Cornelius was sincere in his worshipping of God but he did not have the truth concerning Christ for eternal life. We find in Chapter 11, Verse 14, that God had arranged for Peter to meet with Cornelius and tell him how to be saved:

"Who shall tell thee (Cornelius) words, whereby thou and all thy house shall be saved."

This was God's responsibility and He fulfilled it by sending Peter. When any person has a desire to know the will of God, it then becomes God's responsibility to see that that person hears the Gospel. Cornelius is proof that Romans 1:18 and 19 are true.

B. Many Do Not Desire To Know Christ.

There are also many who do not have a desire to know the truth. It then becomes our responsibility to take the Gospel to them, even when they are not interested in God. We are to persuade them and compel them to come in. Paul reasoned with the Jews in the synagogues many times on his missionary journeys.

Many people do not have a desire to be saved because of a misconception that salvation has to be worked for. Many have come to know Christ as Savior after they have heard the *truth* of the Gospel that we are saved by grace through faith and not by works (Ephesians 2:8,9). You see, it is God's will that *all* would be saved. Romans 1:19,20 remind us that God has manifested in *every person* the knowledge that there is a God. In John 1:9, this light is in every man that is born in the world. Notice again in Verse 7:

"The same come for a witness, to bear witness of the light, that all men *through him might believe."*

These Scriptures reveal to us God's perfect will. The man-made doctrine of election for salvation is in sharp contrast--not in harmony with the will of God and man's free will.

26. Sin--The Condemnation.

"For since by man came death, by man came also the resurrection of the dead. (21)

For as in Adam all die, even so in Christ shall all be made alive." - 1 Corinthians 15:21, 22

The common denominator for all mankind is sin. If God elects some to be saved, and not others, on what basis does God do this? All through the Bible, beginning with Adam, we find that God deals with man according to his sin. God deals with the lost concerning the only sin that He will not forgive and that is the sin of unbelief. Concerning the Christian, God deals with him according to the sin he has in his life *after* he is saved.

Let us go back to the book of Genesis and examine the record concerning the free will of Adam and Eve. In Genesis 2:15-17 we are told:

"And the LORD God took the man, and put him into the garden of Eden to dress it and to keep it. (15)

And the Lord God commanded the man, saying, Of every tree of the garden thou mayest freely eat: (16)

But of the tree of the knowledge of good and evil, thou
shalt not eat of it: for in the day that thou eatest thereof
thou shalt surely die." (17)

At the point when man was created he was not spiritually dead. He was in an untested state concerning the commandment of God. We find no judgment pronounced upon Adam until he purposely, of his own free will, chose to disobey God. God is no respecter of persons. He dealt with Adam and his free will of choice as He does with every offspring of Adam clear on down to you and me. *"For as in Adam all die."* From the time Adam was created until he disobeyed God, he did not possess a fallen nature. He did possess a nature created of God such as <u>no</u> <u>other</u> <u>person</u> <u>has</u> <u>ever</u> <u>had</u>. When he sinned, that fallen nature was passed to every person thereafter. God had known by His foreknowledge that Adam would disobey Him, but He gave Adam the free will to make that decision himself.

It is important to remember that man's destiny of Heaven or Hell is determined by his sin. If a person chooses to pay for his own sin in Hell, God will honor his decision. If one chooses to go to Heaven, then he has the right by trusting God's payment for his sin, which is Jesus Christ. But the choice is theirs. Since everyone has inherited the old sin nature from Adam, God has concluded in Romans 3:23:

"For <u>all</u> have sinned, and come short of the glory of God."

In other words, we do not become a sinner because we sin--we sin because we are born a sinner! Therefore, we fall short of being as righteous as God Himself.

God deals with <u>all</u> mankind on the basis of sin. In Romans 6:23 God has concluded that *"the wages of sin is death."* This is why every person born into this world is in a condemned state. Notice in John 3:17:

135

"For God sent not his Son into the <u>world</u> to condemn the <u>world</u>; but that the <u>world</u> through him might be saved."

We are all condemned because of sin. Notice carefully that justification for eternal life would then be on the basis of God dealing with the sin problem and not because of anything else. When Christ came into the world, the world was already condemned. He did not come to condemn it. But now we see the will of God revealed when He states *"that the <u>world</u> through him might be saved."* God sent Christ to pay for the sins of the <u>world</u>; therefore, any person who wishes may come to Christ and be saved.

God leaves no shroud of darkness surrounding His *<u>purpose</u>* and His *<u>will</u>* concerning man. God very simply tells us *<u>why</u> <u>we</u> <u>are</u> <u>condemned</u>* and *<u>how</u> <u>we</u> <u>can</u> <u>be</u> <u>justified</u>* through our faith in Christ. If God would elect some to be saved, and not others, He would then be a respecter of persons and would contradict His own word as found in Acts 10:34:

"Then Peter opened his mouth, and said, Of a truth I perceive <u>that</u> <u>God</u> <u>is</u> <u>no</u> <u>respecter</u> <u>of persons.</u>"

I would like to continue along on this same line of thought. Notice Jesus' Words in John 14:6:

"...I am the way, the truth, and the life: no man cometh unto the Father, but by me."

In Romans 3:9-11 we find out the indictment of man concerning sin, as this is the basis for God's dealings with mankind. Notice Verses 9 to 11:

"What then? are we better than they? No, in no wise: for we have before proved both Jews and Gentiles, that they are <u>all</u> <u>under</u> <u>sin.</u> (9)

As it is written, There is none righteous, no, not one: (10) There is none that understandeth, there is none that seeketh after God."(11)

Notice again Romans 3:23:

"For all have sinned, and come short of the glory of God."

Now we would like for you to look at Romans 5:12...

"Wherefore as by one man sin entered into the world, and death by sin; and so death passed upon all men, for that all have sinned."

Let us look in the Old Testament at the book of Isaiah in 64:6...

"But we are all as an unclean thing, and all our righteousness are as filthy rags; and we all do fade a leaf; and and our iniquities, like the wind, have taken us away."

Ecclesiastes 7:20 is in perfect harmony with these verses:

"For there is not a just man upon earth, that doeth good, and sinneth not."

Psalms 51:5 speaks concerning David:

"Behold, I was shapen in iniquity; and in sin did my mother conceive me."

In 2 Chronicles 6:36 we are told that...

"If they sin against thee, (for there is no man which sinneth not)."

27. Sin--The Invitation.

It is very important to remember that God deals with all of mankind according to his sin. Notice the invitation that God gives to all mankind as recorded in Isaiah 55:1:

"Ho, every one that thirsteth, come ye to the waters, and he that hath no money; come ye, buy, and eat, yea, come buy wine and milk without money and without price."

Here we are told that God's invitation is extended to everyone. Now let us go to the New Testament in John 1:29:

> "The next day John seeth Jesus coming unto him, and saith, Behold the Lamb of God, which taketh away the sin of the world."

In John 16:8,9 we are told:

> "And when he is come, he will reprove the _world_ of sin, and of righteousness, and of judgment: Of sin, because they believe not on me."

The word _"reprove"_ would be better translated "convict." The Holy Spirit will convict how many? The world. If every person could not be saved, because they were not elected to be saved, then why would the Holy Spirit waste His time convicting those who could not be saved, because they were not elected? Do you begin to see how contradictory this man-invented doctrine of election to salvation is to the Word of God?

Some who endorse election have become very subtle in their endorsement of this doctrine. They seek to appease everyone by their "fence straddling" position. They claim that they do not believe in a limited atonement. They state that God does elect some to be saved, but on the other hand, God did not elect the others to be lost. Those who hold to that position do nothing more than "talk out of both sides of their mouth--which amounts to a big bunch of double-talk!"

When I was in high school a large number of boys went out for the basketball team. After try-outs the coach chose certain boys to remain on the team and cut others. You see, the coach chose to elect certain ones to remain on the team and chose to cut the others. If election to salvation is true, the same principle applies. If God elected some to go to Heaven--then I don't care how you "slice it or cut it"--the others were elected to go to Hell!

Those who endorse this "fence-straddling" position do endorse a limited atonement, they just do not want the title. This is like saying, "I lie--but do not call me a liar," or "I

138

cheat--but do not call me a cheater." Or a person claiming not to believe the Bible but still not wanting to be called an Atheist or Agnostic.

Those who adhere to the doctrine of election to salvation do believe in a limited atonement--whether they claim the title or not! This reveals their dishonesty with themselves and with God's word.

28. Hell

"Then shall he say also unto them on the left hand, Depart from me, ye cursed, into everlasting fire, prepared for the devil and his angels." - Matthew 25:41

God did not prepare Hell for mankind as it was *never God's will* that man should sin. Hell was originally prepared for the devil and his angels. This reveals to us that man had a free will and a free choice. Adam and Eve, the progenitors of the human race, chose willfully to disobey God, which they did. God did not elect them to do that. It was of their own volition to choose or reject the will of God. So it is with everyone to choose or reject God's payment for their sin, the Lord Jesus Christ. Everyone stands responsible for their own decision.

29. The Twelve Spies Sent To Canaan

We find the record in Numbers 13. God had promised the land of Canaan to the children of Israel in Verse 2. Twelve spies were sent into Canaan and returned with their report. Two men, Caleb and Joshua, gave an encouraging report and stated in Verse 30:

"...Let us go up at once, and possess it..."

139

The other Ten gave a negative report of discouragement in Verse 31:

> *"...We be not able to go up against the people; for they are stronger than we."*

The Ten went against God's will because of their <u>lack of faith</u>. If they were elected to serve with no free will, they would never have gone against God's will. Either God elected them to go against His own will or they, themselves, chose to oppose God's will. Would one dare place the blame on God for their disobedience or should we hold the Ten responsible for their own choice? This author's verdict is: God is innocent--the ten spies are guilty!

30. Israel's Murmuring

Israel was about to rebel by refusing to enter Canaan and claim it as their possession. They were persuaded by the negative report of the ten spies. Caleb and Joshua pleaded with them in Verse 9:

> *"Only <u>rebel</u> <u>not</u> ye against the LORD, neither fear ye the people of the land; for they are bread for us; their defense is departed from them, and the LORD is with us: fear them not."*

Why plead with them to <u>rebel not</u> if they had no free will to rebel with? Here, again, man stands responsible for his decisions by his own free will and choice.

Satan is very pleased with his success in attacking the character of God by falsely accusing Him of choosing, or electing some for Heaven and some for Hell. God shouts from Heaven by His Word, the Bible. "Read John 8:44, where I told you Satan is a murderer and a liar!" God refutes Satan's lies as He states in 2 Peter 3:9 that He is *"...not willing that any should perish, but that all should come to repentance* (i.e., Gr. "a change of mind")." WHY?

> *"For God so loved the world, that he gave his only begotten Son, that whosoever believeth in him should not perish, but have everlasting life." - John 3:16*

There are thousands of examples that could be added. This section contains only the tip of the iceberg; but, I feel, enough to stimulate ones thinking. God gives you a free will to choose your own destiny; Heaven, or Hell.

> *"He that believeth on the Son hath everlasting life: and he that believeth not the Son shall not see life; but the wrath of God abideth on him." - John 3:36*

"False Doctrine Shipwrecks Souls"

"Hyper-Calvinism is unscriptural, false doctrine. It tends to flourish in intellectual pride and in neglect of soul winning, and is a symptom of moral guilt. It is Satan's effort to kill concern and compassion for souls."

- Dr. John R. Rice, Founder of *Sword of the Lord*

"False Doctrine Shipwrecks Souls"

CHAPTER FOUR

EXHIBITING VERSES ENDORSING MAN'S FREE WILL

1. Robot's Have No Free Will

If God had elected certain people to be saved and to serve with no free will, then all of the saved would be like robots. They would be programmed, with no thinking ability of their own. In Genesis 1:27 we are told:

> *"So God created man in his own <u>image</u>, in the <u>image</u> of God created he him; male and female created he them."*

This is not referring to God's physical image, as God is spirit; but, rather, to one's personality, mind, will, emotions, intellect and etc. *If God created certain people with no free will--then God had no free will, as they were created in the image of God!*

God wants us to love Him because He first loves us. How could God be satisfied with a love He, Himself, had to program into those whom He elected to save. This kind of love would be artificial--not real. God's will is that we love Him out of our free will that he gave us.

2. Is God Unrighteous?

Can God Be just and righteous in electing some to be saved and not others? The answer is NO! Notice in Romans 3:26:

> *"To declare, I say, at this time his righteousness: that he might be just, and the justifier of him which believeth in Jesus."*

God could not be just and righteous if He elected some for salvation, and not others. You see, the "doctrine of election" makes God unjust and unrighteous; but the free will of man exalts His justice and righteousness, because anyone can be saved if they so choose.

3. Is God Guilty Of Sinning Against His Own Word?

God is <u>not</u> a respecter of persons. The Lord wills that we follow His example and not be a respecter of persons, which is sin. In James 2:9 we are told:

> *"But if ye have respect of persons, ye commit sin, and are convinced of the law as transgressors."*

God loves humanity with a greater love (Greek, agape) than we can ever experience until we are saved. Then we have the divine nature (2 Peter 1:4) implanted within us. Many times it is hard, naturally, to love a person with their bad habits, attitudes, insults and etc. This can only be done through the Holy Spirit which enables us to love that person in spite of their character, the way God loved us before we were saved.

Since God expects us not to have respect of persons, it would discredit the character of God for Him to elect some to be saved and reject others. Since it would be sin for us to show partiality, then God would be guilty of the same if election were true. In other words, God would be instructing

144

us not to do something and then be guilty of doing it Himself. How absurd! Notice Peter's words in Acts 10:34:

"Then Peter opened his mouth, and said, Of a truth I perceive that God is no respecter of persons."

It now becomes your choice, either to believe *God's Word*- -or election predicated upon the philosophy of men.

"It is better to trust in the Lord than to put confidence in man." - Psalm 118:8

4. God's Will For The Abundant Life.

"The thief cometh not, but for to steal, and to kill, and to destroy; I am come that they might have life, and that they might have it more abundantly." - John 10:10

Since it is God's will that the Christian have an abundant life, then why would God wait until some people are much older before saving them? If God has already predetermined and elected some to be saved, then why would He not do it at a very young age? That way they could enjoy being a Christian all of their life instead of maybe the last few years of their life.

In other words, why would God allow a person to waste his life when he could be using it for the Lord if he was saved at an early age? Many drunkards have been saved and still carry the results of that sin with cirrhosis of the liver. Many homes have been broken up because of the parents practicing sin in their lives. Yet, many of these people are saved after one or two divorces. If they were elected to be saved anyway, why would God not have spared them all of this heartache by saving them at an early age?

Remember, in John 10:10 it was God's will that we have life and have it abundantly. The "doctrine of election" fades into oblivion when examined under the light of God's Word. The Word of God is like a refiner's fire. In the steel mills, extreme heat is used to melt the steel so the impurities will come to the surface. In like manner, the Word of God is a refiner's fire which brings to the surface the impurities of this false doctrine.

5. John 3:15-18 - God Loves Everyone He Created.

"That <u>whosoever</u> believeth in him should not perish, but have eternal life. (15) For God so loved the <u>world</u>, that he gave His only begotten Son, that <u>whosoever</u> believeth in him should not perish, but have everlasting life. (16)

For God sent not his Son into the <u>world</u> to condemn the <u>world</u>; but that the <u>world</u> through him might be saved. (17)

He that believeth on him is not condemned: but he that believeth not is condemned already, because he has not believed in the name of the only begotten Son of God." (18)

The word *"world"* reveals God's will that all be saved. The word *"whosoever"* is the opportunity for every man to be saved.

The whole context of these verses are that a person is guilty and condemned because they, themselves, choose not to believe in the name of the only begotten Son of God. These Scriptures are very simple and easy to understand, showing us the will of God and the responsibility of man. Any person can be saved. It is God's will that all be saved, but the choice is entirely up to the discretion of the individual.

6. John 4:13-14 - God Invites All To Heaven.

"Jesus answered and said unto her, <u>whosoever</u> drinketh of this water shall thirst again: But <u>whosoever</u> drinketh of the water that I shall give him shall never thirst; but the

water that I shall give him shall be in him a well of water springing up into everlasting life."

Those who endorse election to salvation seem to overlook the word "whosoever." The election people very subtly emphasize two statements that appear in Verse 14:

"I shall give him..."

They claim this endorses God's choosing or electing some to be saved. They claim only those who are saved are to whom Christ gives this water. This is the error they make by extracting certain phrases and not adhering to the whole verse. You will notice that Christ <u>offers</u> the living water, but does not <u>make</u> a person drink. You see, Christ offers the water to anyone, but only those who choose to drink of it will have everlasting life. Verse 15 makes this perfectly clear:

"The woman saith unto him, Sir, give me this water, that I thirst not, neither come hither to draw."

The woman wanted what Christ had to offer. Here Christ is using literal water, metaphorically, concerning His Word. Maybe you are reading this book and have a thirst for everlasting life? You may, right now, put your trust in Jesus Christ--believing that He died on the cross to pay for your sins. In so doing, you have drunk of the water that Christ offered, by faith, which insures you of receiving God's promise of everlasting life.

7. John 4:41-42 - Many Believed.

"And many more believed because of his own word; And said unto the woman, Now we believe, not because of thy saying: for we have heard him ourselves, and know that this is indeed the Christ, <u>the Saviour of the world</u>."

Our first question is--"If election were true, why did not all of the people believe on Christ after hearing the testimony of the Samaritan woman?" Notice in Verse 39:

147

*"And many of the Samaritans of that city believed on
him for the saying of the woman, which testified, He told me
that all ever I did."*

There were many who believed on Christ because of the
Samaritan woman's testimony. In Verses 41 and 42 we are
told that many believed when they heard Christ himself, but
would not believe just by hearing the woman's testimony. If
they were elected to be saved, then why would they not
believe the testimony of the Samaritan woman? The election
people state that "whom God had elected possessed irresistible
grace"; therefore, how could they have resisted the testimony
of the Samaritan woman if they were elected to be saved?

One may reason that, "Well, they were not saved because
they would only believe if they heard Christ himself." If that
line of reasoning were true, then no one would be saved today
because Christ is not here personally, Himself. But in Romans
10:17 the Word of God tells us that:

*"...faith cometh by hearing, and hearing by the word of
God."*

If election to salvation were true, then all that heard the
testimony of the Samaritan woman would have been unable to
resist that word and would have believed. But such is not the
case.

The second point of interest is found in Verse 42:

*"...for we have heard him ourselves, and know that this
is indeed the Christ, the <u>Saviour</u> <u>of</u> <u>the</u> <u>world.</u>"*

It does not say "Saviour of the elect" but "Saviour of the
world." It is God's will that all be saved. If God elected some
to be saved, and not others, He would be going against His
own will--which would be impossible.

8. John 5:23 - If "All Men" can Honor the Son, Then "All" Can Believe.

"That all men should honour the Son, even as they honour the Father. He that honoureth not the Son honoureth not the Father which hath sent him."

Since it is God's will that all should honor Christ, He would be going against His own will if He chose some to be saved and not others. In Verse 24 the verse is given to all:

"Verily, verily, I say unto you, he that heareth my word, and believeth on him that sent me, hath everlasting life, and shall not come into condemnation; but is passed from death unto life."

In Verse 24, "he hath" is equivalent and complimentary to the "all men" in Verse 23. These verses deal another death-blow to the philosophy of election for salvation.

9. John 6:51 - Christ Invites "Any Man" To Believe

"I am the living bread which came down from heaven: if any man eat of this bread, he shall live forever: and the bread that I will give is my flesh, which I will give for the life of the world."

It does not take a theologian to understand that Christ invites *"any man"* to believe on Him, and that He gave His life for the world! This verse is just another nail sealing the lid of the coffin which contains the heretical doctrine of election.

Let us look at Verse 54 which is complimentary to Verse 51:

"Whoso eateth my flesh, and drinketh my blood, hath eternal life: and I will raise him up at the last day."

You see, when Scripture agrees with Scripture, there is not even the slightest crack where false doctrine can seep through! This is why it is so important for Christians to study their Bibles and not just sit in church on Sunday mornings listening to a sermon and never opening the pages of God's Word.

10. John 8:24 - "If ye," Someone With A Choice.

"I said therefore unto you, that ye shall die in your sins: for if ye believe not that I am He, ye shall die in your sins."

Notice the words *"if ye believe not."* These words show us that a person has a free will and choice. "If ye" (your choice) eliminates "elected" (someone with no choice). Here, again, is illuminated the free will of man.

11. John 11:25, 26. - "Whosoever...Believeth"

"Jesus said unto her, I am the resurrection, and the life: he that believeth in me, though he were dead, yet shall he live: (25) And whosoever liveth and believeth in me shall never die. Believest thou this?" (26)

The *"whosoever"* in Verse 26 is equivalent to *"he that"* in Verse 25. These verses reveal to us that man's free will and responsibility stand erect on the solid foundation of God's Word as election crumbles on the sinking sands of philosophy. (Colossians 2:8)

12. John 12:46-48 - "Whosoever" Means The World!

"I am come a light into the world, that whosoever believeth on me should not abide in darkness. (46) And if any man here my words, and believe not, I judge him not: for I came not to judge the world, but to save the world. (47) He that rejecteth me, and receiveth not my words, hath one that judgeth him: the word that I have spoken, the same shall judge him in the last day." (48)

These verses reveal the will of God, which is to save the world. The free will of man is clearly seen in God's invitation

150

to *"whosoever."* God's will was clearly stated when the Bible said that Christ came to *"save the world."*

If election to salvation were true, here is the dilemma we would find as we compare election philosophy with these verses. Let us analyze the situation. God wants to save the world. The Word of God is given which will judge a person if they reject it. God would then, purposely, hinder and restrict a person from believing the Word He gave them. Then He would, further, judge that person worthy of Hell with the same Word he restricted them from believing. Why? Because they were not elected for salvation!

We are then told that we cannot understand this! I might confirm, at this point, that this is absolutely true. The reason we cannot understand it is because it is understandably untrue! One cannot understand something that God is accused of which God did not do. This is the result of twisting and turning the Word of God to make it fit their doctrine, instead of taking the clear teaching of God's Word that states "He came to light every person in the world." Verse 47 states that He came to *"save the world."* Therefore, the reasoning of the predestinationalist would be totally against the Word, character and righteousness of God, Himself.

13. Acts 2:21 - "Whosoever" Means "Anyone."

> *"And it shall come to pass that whosoever shall call on the name of the Lord shall be saved."*

"Whosoever" means anyone who wishes to do so. The same invitation appears in two other places, Joel 2:32 and Romans 10:13. As we continue in Acts 2, we find out that Peter was speaking to the Jews on the Day of Pentecost and in Verses 22 and 23 we are told:

> *"Ye men of Israel, hear these words; Jesus and Nazareth, a man approved of God among you by miracles and wonders and signs, which God did by him in the midst of you, as ye*

yourselves also know: (22) him, being delivered by the determinate counsel and foreknowledge of God, ye have taken, and by <u>wicked</u> hands have crucified and slain." (23)

How could God say they had *"wicked hands"* when He predestinated them to do what they did? If that were true, then it would be God Himself who had wicked hands!

Here we can see the folly of predestination. Keep in mind that Peter is addressing those Jews on the day of Pentecost who had rejected Christ and yet, in Verse 21, he advises this same group:

"And it shall come to pass that <u>whosoever</u> shall call on the name of the Lord shall be saved."

Even though they had crucified Christ over a month-and-a-half previously, they could still be saved--they could still change their minds and believe on the Lord Jesus Christ and be saved.

As we look at Acts 2:41, we find there were about 3,000 who put their trust in Christ after hearing Peter preach.

"Then they that gladly received his word were baptized: and the same day there were added unto them about three thousand souls."

Our point is simply this, if God had predestinated them to be saved--then why were they not saved when they heard Christ, Himself, preaching? Why, after all the evidence that was given to them by signs and miracles, would they not have believed that Christ was their Messiah--especially if they were predestinated to do so. In other words, they could have resisted the grace that Christ offered to them, which was-- Himself, as payment for their sins. You see, they had all the proof that anyone would ever need by the miracles that were done, as Peter reminds them in Verse 22 of this chapter. If they were elected to be saved, then why were they not saved when hearing Christ, Himself. No, one can easily see that election to salvation is not a Biblical doctrine; but, rather a sectarian philosophy of Satanic origin.

14. Acts 17:30 - God Commands "All Men" To Change Their Minds About Christ.

> *"And the times of this ignorance God winked at: but now <u>commandeth</u> <u>all</u> <u>men</u> everywhere to repent"* *(Change your mind).*

God commands *all men,* everywhere to change their minds and come to Christ by faith. Now notice Verse 31:

> *"Because he hath appointed a day, in the which He will judge the <u>world</u> in righteousness by that man whom he hath ordained; whereof he hath given assurance unto <u>all</u> men, in that he hath raised him from the dead."*

My question is, "Why would God give assurance unto <u>all</u> men if all men could not be saved?" The reason He gives assurance unto all men that Christ has risen from the dead is because of God's will in Verse 30 that *"...<u>all</u> <u>men</u>"* repent." Notice in Verse 31 that God will *"judge the world in righteousness."* How could God be a righteous judge if He elected some to be saved and not others? He would, then, become unrighteous! God's will is clearly revealed so that everyone can understand. It is the philosophical reasoning of the predestinationalists that becomes obscure, not the Word of God.

15. Galatians 5:4 - Some Men Choose To Be Justified By The Law.

> *"Christ is become of no effect unto you, <u>whosoever</u> of you are justified by the law; ye are fallen from grace."*

There were those in Galatia who were trying to be justified by circumcision and the keeping of the law. Notice in Verse 2:

153

> *"Behold, I Paul say unto you, that* if ye *be circumcised, Christ shall profit you nothing."*

This was their choice, but it was not God's will. Again, the *"whosoever"* in Verse 4 stands out. It was *their* will. They had chosen to be justified by the law rather than being justified through Jesus Christ. John 14:6 tells us there is only one way to God and that is through Christ:

> *"Jesus saith unto him, I am the way, the truth, and the life: no man cometh unto the Father, but by me."*

When you sweep away all of the debris from the cult religions, you will see a self-righteous, works salvation coming to the surface. The "whosoever" in Verse 4 reveals that it is the free will of any individual to be justified by grace or by works. God holds each person responsible for the decisions they make.

If election were true and God overpowers the free will of man, then it would have been useless to have Galatians 5:1 in the Bible.

> *"Stand fast therefore in the liberty wherewith Christ hath made us free, and be not entangled again with the yoke of bondage."*

If we have no free will, then it would have been needless to ask the Christian to "stand fast" and to "be not entangled again." If election were true, they would have never had a will to do so.

16. Matthew 24:14 - The Gospel Is For The "World."

> *"And this gospel of the kingdom shall be preached in all the world for a witness to all nations; and then shall the end come."*

This Scripture is in reference to the 7-Year Tribulation Period in which, again, the whole world will be reached with the Gospel. Even by the end of the first century, the gospel had been preached to the whole world (Read Romans 1:8, Romans 10:18, and Colossians 1:6,23). You will find from Genesis to Revelation that God's will is for everyone to be saved. That is the reason for the Gospel being taken to the world.

17. Matthew 11:28, 29 - "The Invitation Is To "All."

> "Come unto me, all ye that labour and are heavy laden, and I will give you rest. (28) Take my yoke upon you, and learn of me; for I am meek and lowly of heart: and ye shall find rest unto your souls." (29)

This is for salvation that the invitation is universal. This is the purpose of the Holy Spirit--to convict the world of sin, righteousness and judgment. (See John 16:7-11) Any student of the Bible recognizes that Verse 28 is speaking about salvation and Verse 29 is speaking concerning our service to the Lord. The invitation is to everyone, and we thank God for that. Since everyone is invited, everyone has a right to accept or reject Christ. Again, the free will of man is brought forth.

18. 1 Timothy 4:10 - Christ Is The Savior Of "All Men."

> "For therefore we both labour and suffer reproach, because we trust in the living God, who is the Saviour of all men, specially of those that believe. These things command and teach."

Here we see that Christ is the Savior of "all men," especially of those that believe, He died for the sins of the world and He wants to be the Savior of every person born. He is only the Savior, specifically and personally, to those who choose Him by their own free will. Again, we are grateful to God that His will is "that none should perish, but that all should repent (i.e. change their mind)." The forgiveness of sins will only be appropriated to those who accept Him as their Savior.

155

These Scriptures are so clear and specific that an explanation is hardly needed. Since God's will is to be the Savior of all men, a person would have no one to blame but themselves if they die, and spend eternity in Hell. That person would have to go against God's will and reject Him out of their own free will.

19. Hebrews 2:9 - Christ Died For "Every Man."

"But we see Jesus, who was made a little lower than the angels for the suffering of death, crowned with glory and honour; that he by the grace of God should <u>taste</u> <u>death</u> <u>for</u> <u>every</u> <u>man.</u>"

Here is another verse in support of man's free will and declaring God's will. What can be added to "Christ tasted death for *every man?*" Please do not ask me to believe Christ contradicted Himself by tasting death for every man and then electing only some to believe!

Those that support predestination concerning salvation actually accuse God of not loving all of mankind, even though it is never admitted. It is hard to imagine anyone trying to accuse God of electing some to go to Heaven but not others, then saying "We just cannot understand it." Of course they cannot! It is simply not true.

20. 1 Timothy 2:5,6 - Christ Is the "Ransom For All."

"For there is one God, and one mediator between God and men, the man Christ Jesus; (5) Who gave himself a ransom for <u>all</u>, *to be testified in due time." (6)*

This Scripture is perfectly clear, stating that Christ paid the price for sin for everyone. If someone was predestinated for Hell, why would God send His Son, Christ, to be ransom for those who were predestinated to Hell? This, of course, does not make sense. God proved His love by giving Christ as a ransom for all. Each one of us now stands responsible for the choice we make because of the free will God has given to each of us.

21. 2 Peter 3:9 - The Lord Is..."Not Willing Any Should Perish."

"The Lord is not slack concerning his promise, as some men count slackness; but is longsuffering to us-ward, not willing that any should perish, but that all should come to repentance" (i.e. A change of mind).

Those who endorse predestination and election to salvation will have to accuse God of lying in this verse. Yet God is so clear and precise in His teachings that there is no excuse for a misunderstanding. These verses reveal to us the direct mind and will of God concerning salvation.

The predestinationalists say they believe this verse, but the doctrine they endorse reveals otherwise. Instead of accepting the Word of God for what it says, they insert their meaning, their doctrine, and then justify it by declaring "We cannot understand the mind of God." This is the same double-talk that is used by cult religions.

For example, Jehovah's Witnesses say they believe that Jesus Christ is the Savior of the world. What they mean by what they say is entirely different from what the Scriptures teach. When they declare that they believe Jesus is the Savior of the world, they mean that He is a good man, not that He is God in human flesh. Therefore, He is the Savior of the world by the example He sets for us to follow.

This double-talk is nothing more than following the example of Christ and by good works we can merit our salvation. Of course, this is contrary to the Word of God because no one will ever go to Heaven on their own righteousness. The point we want to make is, they make the same claims as we do, but their meaning is entirely different.

Predestinationalists say they believe these verses, but their meaning is entirely foreign to the Word of God. Again, I want to emphasize that the doctrine of predestination for salvation is not some "mini-doctrine." It is a damnable doctrine because it attacks the will of God as clearly stated in His Word, it attacks the righteousness of God, it makes God a respecter of persons which is totally against God's Word. When God says in 2nd Peter 3:9 that He is *"not willing that any should perish,"* that is exactly what God means!

22. 1 Timothy 2:3,4 - "God... Will Have All Men To Be Saved."

"For this is good and acceptable in the sight of God our Savior; who will have all men to be saved, and to come unto the knowledge of the truth."

The predestinationalists tell us they do not understand how God can say this and yet elect some to Heaven and not others to Hell. Not understanding is the result of not taking God at His Word. When a person takes a word such as "predestinate, elect, or choose," quotes it out of context, does not correlate it with other Scripture concerning the same subject, then mixes it together with humanistic reasoning and wisdom, you have produced a batch of philosophy that is impossible to understand. How easy it is to believe the Word of God that states His will is to *"have all men to be saved."*

23. 1 John 2:2 - The "Whole World" Means The "Whole World!"

"And he is the propitiation (payment) for our sins: and not for ours only, but also for the sins of the whole world."

Any person can be saved as the sins of everyone have been paid for by the death of Christ on Calvary. God has extended to man the free will and right to choose his own destiny. Therefore, he stands totally responsible for his acceptance or rejection of the Lord Jesus Christ. The "whole world" means the "whole world!"

24. 1 John 5:1 - "Whosoever Believeth."

"Whosoever believeth that Jesus is the Christ is born of God."

"Whosoever" reveals the free will of all mankind. Did God make a mistake? Should He have written "the elect that believeth?" Is the philosophy of election in error, or is God?

"It is better to trust in the Lord than to put confidence in man." - Psalm 118:8

25. 2 John 9 - "Whosoever" Can Choose To Transgress.

"Whosoever transgresseth, and abideth not in the doctrine of Christ, hath not God. He hath abideth in the doctrine of Christ, he hath both the Father and the Son."

Here, again, we have projected to us the right of man to transgress *"and abideth not in the doctrine of Christ."* A person has the right to abide or abide not in the doctrine of Christ-- this is that person's free will. God has given man a free will to accept or reject Him. The "whosoever" is a person's right and free will to accept or reject Christ.

26. Hebrews 10:26 - Sinning "Willfully" Brings Consequences.

"For it we sin willfully after that we have received the knowledge of the truth, there remaineth no more sacrifice for sins."

The point of this verse is--that we *sin willfully*. It is our choice. If election to salvation were true, how can one sin willfully? If one were elected to salvation and elected to serve Christ, then it would be impossible for him to sin willfully. If election to salvation were true, we would have to do what we were elected to do. This would be against the whole character

159

and purpose of God for His children, as well as the lost. Since we sin *willfully*, of our own accord, we must bear our own responsibility before God for our decisions.

27. Revelation 22:17-19 - Whosoever = Every Man = Any Man.

"And the Spirit and the bride say, Come. And let him that heareth say, Come. And let him that is athirst come. And whosoever will, let him take the water of life freely. (17)

For I testify unto every man that heareth the words of the prophecy of this book, If any man shall add unto these things, God shall add unto him the plagues that are written in this book: (18)

And if any man shall take away from the words of the book of this prophecy, God shall take away his part out of the book of life, and out of the holy city, and from the things which are written in this book. (19)

In Verse 17 the free will of man stands out. *"Whosoever will may take of the water of life freely."* Then God testifies to *every man* what will happen to *any man* who takes away from His Word. This, of course, places the responsibility upon *any man.* Then in Verse 19, *"If any man shall take away from the words of the book of this prophecy"*, and He states what will happen. The point I am stressing is, it is man's free will and God emphasizes that all the way through His Word.

Let me give an example of what one can do with Scripture if they follow the same pattern of interpretation as the predestinationalists. They "lasso" one Scripture and tie it up whenever they come to the words "elect, choosing, foreknowledge, and predestination. Then they saddle their "hobby-horse" and use it to over-ride the free will of man. They disregard all other Scripture which invites all men to be saved.

Here is the same extreme to which you could go with other portions of God's Word. In Acts 27:31 we are told:

> *"Paul said to the centurion and to the soldiers, except these abide in the ship, ye cannot be saved."*

Taken alone, this would mean that we would all have to abide in a ship somewhere on order to be saved. I know that sounds absolutely ridiculous, and in reality, it is. But in the same sense, that is exactly how predestinationalists build their false doctrine. They yank one Scripture out that has the word "elect, foreknowledge, or choosing" without applying it in the context or correlating it with other Scripture. All false doctrine is built upon this same procedure. We are told in 2 Timothy 2:15:

> *"Study to shew thyself approved unto God, a workman that needeth not to be ashamed, rightly dividing the word of truth."*

That means being _honest_ with God's Word. Correct interpretation, evaluation and doctrine is a result of relating all Scriptures that pertain to a certain subject, person, or doctrine. When those verses complement each other and totally agree, then you have the correct interpretation and doctrine.

You see, God is not divided nor does He contradict Himself. Only men contradict themselves. This is done when they attempt to build a doctrine upon a particular Scripture or word that is in direct contrast to other portions of Scriptures.

Are you aware that the Bible says *"There is no God?"* This is recorded in Psalms 14:1. But that is only part of the verse, not all of the verse. The entire verse reads...

"The fool hath said in his heart, there is no God. They are corrupt, they have done abominable works, there is none that doeth good."

Do you see what men can do by only using part of God's word and not all of it. You will always come out with the right doctrine when all Scriptures agree concerning a certain subject, as the mind of God is not confused, nor contradictory.

28. Galatians 1:13,14 - God's Timing Is Perfect - Paul's Was Not!

"For ye have heard of my conversation in time past in the Jews' religion, how that beyond measure I persecuted the church of God, and wasted it: (13) And profited in the Jews' religion above many of my equals in mine own nation, being more exceedingly zealous of the traditions of my fathers."
(14)

Notice Acts 8:1 concerning Saul in reference to the death of Stephen:

"And Saul was consenting unto his death. And at that time there was a great persecution against the church which was at Jerusalem; and they were all scattered abroad throughout the regions of Judaea and Samaria, except the apostles."

If God had elected Paul to be saved--so that he had no choice of his own--then why would He not bring Paul to a knowledge of Christ prior to the time of his participation in the persecution and killing of many, many Christians? How many Christians Paul killed, we do not know. It could have been hundreds and hundreds that Paul not only persecuted and wasted; but, actually slaughtered and murdered.

Would the predestinationalists tell me that God allowed him to do this when He had already elected him to be saved? If Paul had been elected to salvation, could not God have saved Paul prior to this and Paul could have been winning souls to Christ instead of killing Christians? Again, we find that "election to salvation" is against the will of God. Satan loves this false doctrine as it deceives many people into thinking that God saw a speck of good in them; therefore, he elected them and gave them the faith to believe with.

29. 1 John, Chapter 1, Man's Free Will Illuminated.

Any student of the Bible recognizes the difference between sonship and fellowship (being obedient to the Lord after we are saved). 1st John 1 is dealing with the believer's fellowship with Christ and other Christians. Notice his free will.

Free Will to Lie: Verse 6 - *"If we say that we have fellowship with him, and walk in darkness, we lie, and do not tell the truth."*

Free Will to Obey: Verse 7 - *"But if we walk in the light (obedience) ...we have fellowship one with another..."*

Free Will to Deceive Ourselves: Verse 8 - *"If we say we have no sin, we deceive ourselves, and the truth is not in us."*

Free Will to Confess: Verse 9 - *"If we confess our sin, he is faithful and just to forgive us our sins..."*

Free Will to Deny We Have Sinned: Verse 10 - *"If we say that we have not sinned, we make him a liar, and his word is not in us."*

These verses stress the believer's free will. *"If we"* is used four times, and *"But if"* is used once. If election were true, then the possibility would never exist for a Christian to lie (Verse 6), deceive themselves (Verse 8), or make God a liar (Verse 10). In Verse 9, *"If we confess our sin"* would seem a bit confusing. According to Nettleton on page 22, "His saved ones serve Him." If Christians are elected to serve with no free will to do otherwise, where did the sin they are confessing in Verse 9 come from? The confusion either lies with God or with Nettleton.

Now, you have a choice! As for me, I choose to believe God's Word, not the philosophy of some man. God warns the Christian to beware of deceitful men.

> *"Beware lest any man spoil you through philosophy and vain deceit, after the tradition of men, after the rudiments of the world, and not after Christ."* - Colossians 2:8

"False Doctrine Shipwrecks Souls"

God does not "decide" who will be saved. God does not "make" anyone believe, even though He *wants* all to believe and be saved. But God, since He can see the future, knows who will believe and who will not believe. Long before I was ever born, God knew I would decide to trust Christ as my Saviour. But this "foreknowledge" of His did not CAUSE me to trust Christ as my Saviour. -

Dr. A. Ray Stanford.

"False Doctrine Shipwrecks Souls"

" To open their eyes, and to turn them from darkness to light, and from the power of Satan unto God, that they may receive forgiveness of sins, and inheritance among them which are sanctified by faith that is in me." - Acts 26:18

"False Doctrine Shipwrecks Souls"

CHAPTER FIVE

EXPOSING NETTLETON'S STATEMENTS & PHILOSOPHY

Answering Statements By Those Who Endorse Election

Mr. Nettleton, in endorsing election, asks me to believe his terminology instead of God's. This is a little hard to comprehend, since the same author keeps suggesting that we must stand on the Scriptures and let the Bible speak for Itself. Here is what he says on page 21 (*Chosen to Salvation*):

"For the purpose of clarity, let us use the term 'foreseen faith'. Since the word 'foreknowledge' is an ambiguous word in the theological realm."

After supplying his own terminology, because to him "foreknowledge" is an ambiguous word, he takes it upon himself to give us his definition of "foreknowledge" on the same page (21). His statement is:

"The word 'foreknowledge' means fullness of knowledge which indicates intimacy of relationship. 'Foreknowledge' therefore is the knowing of personal relationship rather than the knowing of facts. Study Acts 2:23, Romans 8:29 and Romans 11:2. Be careful before you interpret 'foreknowledge' as mere familiarity with facts."

It is amazing to me that Mr. Nettleton attests that foreknowledge is an unclear word in the theological realm but he, himself, has the true insight to define the word for us.

In the *Expository Dictionary of New Testament Words* by W.E. Vine, "foreknowledge" is the Greek verb "prognosko." "Pro" is "before," "gnosko" is "to know" and is used only of divine knowledge. It is, very simply, one of God's attributes--His omniscience. That is, He knows everything that is going to happen before it happens! For one to state that "foreknowledge" is the knowing of personal relationship <u>rather</u> than the knowing of facts, is a subtle attempt to extract and emphasize a part of God's omniscience so it can fit a particular doctrine. No, God's omniscience cannot be divided, for He knows the facts concerning what is going to happen in the future--concerning *everything*.

Since God is dealing with people on His earth, His foreknowledge is not limited to only knowing who will believe in Christ; but, indeed, knowing every fact about every person's life. The above statement that foreknowledge was pertaining to personal relationship rather than the facts was the author's foundation to his readers as he prepared them for his next step in influencing them towards election to salvation. The next step being (page 23):

"The fact stands that God planned to save certain individuals, planned the means of faith..."

This statement indicates to me that God will even give you the faith to believe with, so that your salvation is attributed to the sovereign election of God and you have no free will of your own. We challenge this philosophy with the Word of God as given in 2 Peter 3:9:

"The Lord is not slack concerning his promise, as some men count slackness; but is longsuffering to us-ward, not willing that any should perish, but that <u>all</u> should come to repentance."

I am told that I should accept God's election by faith since God did not see fit to tell me why He chose some and rejected others. I am glad that it is man that asks me to accept this philosophy instead of God, because the God I know is not a God of confusion! My God has explained:

1. What Christ Did.

"For God so loved the world, that he gave his only begotten Son, that whosoever believeth in him should not perish, but have everlasting life." - John 3:16

2. Why He Did It.

"But God commendeth his love toward us, in that, while we were yet sinners, Christ died for us." - Romans 5:8

3. Where I Stand.

"For all have sinned, and come short of the glory of God." - Romans 3:23

4. What I Can Do.

"And brought them out, and said, Sirs, what must I do to be saved? (30) And they said, Believe on the Lord Jesus Christ, and thou shalt be saved, and thy house." - Acts 16:30, 31

Yes, anyone can be saved. A man told me once that this man's whole house was saved because they were elected to be saved. Of course, the Word of God does <u>not</u> say that. Notice Verse 32 of Acts 16:

"And they spoke unto him the word of the Lord, and to <u>all</u> that were in his house."

You will notice that they all heard the Word of God. Romans 10:17 tells us that:

"...Faith cometh by hearing and hearing by the word of God."

169

Now notice Acts 16:34:

"And when he had brought them into his house, he set meat before them, and rejoiced, <u>believing</u> <u>in</u> <u>God</u> <u>WITH</u> <u>all</u> <u>his</u> <u>house.</u>"

No one was elected to be saved, but everyone in that house that heard the Word of God chose to believe on the Lord Jesus Christ. I know many families where the " whole house" is saved. Mine is one example. Not all at the same time, but they are now all saved and, for that, I am thankful! I know many, many families where everyone in the family is saved. Because a whole family is saved does not mean they were elected to be saved. It does mean that everyone in the family chose, out of their own their own free will, to put their trust in the Lord Jesus Christ as their personal Savior.

Yes, one can easily reconcile the sovereignty of God, the foreknowledge of God and the free will of man. The sovereignty of God meaning that God is independent of anyone else. God can do anything He wishes to do <u>EXCEPT</u> contradict Himself, lie, be unfaithful to His Word, etc. For His veracity is at stake. The whole character of God would be in jeopardy if God elected some to be saved, and not others, after stating in John 3:16 that:

"For God so loved the <u>WORLD</u>...that <u>WHOSOEVER</u> believeth in him should not perish, but have everlasting life."

God does not say one thing and do another, or He would be a liar! In Titus 1:2 we are reminded that, "God cannot lie." In Hebrews 6:18 we find that it *"was impossible for God to lie."* When comparing the doctrine of election to salvation with the Word of God, we find it is contrary to every aspect of the character of God, the nature of God, the holiness and veracity of God. I choose to anchor my faith in God's Word,

"Let God be true but every man a liar" (Romans 3:4).

170

You see, foreknowledge does not include the element of choosing or electing certain ones to be saved; therefore, it does not impede the free will of man. God has fulfilled His responsibility as far as paying for the sins of the world. He will continue to convict with the Holy Spirit, but, ultimately, our destiny lies within our own hands. The price has been paid. It is our choice whether we will accept it or reject it. We are totally responsible for our own destinies as God's will is that none should perish.

Statements By Nettleton Examined And Answered

The following statements are taken from Mr. Nettleton's book entitled *"Chosen to Salvation."* We have selected a few statements, paragraphs and verses which Mr. Nettleton uses to support his position on the doctrine of election. What is most interesting and worthy of examination are the verses--or pieces of verses--that are used in support of his position. We are going to look at these verses in their context and determine if they have been properly applied.

1. Wrong Application.

On pages 13 and 14 of Nettleton's book he states:

"There are two things man will never understand this side of Heaven: how God could elect to save some sinners and not others, and how He could make man responsible for his faith and unbelief. Our minds are too small and too perverted by sin. Our knowledge is so limited, not only because God has revealed only a limited amount of truth; but also because we have not availed ourselves of all that has been revealed. We are not prejudiced in favor of ourselves as men. We are prone to pattern God after ourselves. We create God in our own image and likeness. God rebukes our thoughts as He says, '...Thou thoughtest that I was altogether such an one as thyself...' (Psalms 50:21)."

171

Psalm 50:21 is used by Nettleton as a little slap to Christians who would dare to oppose his position on election, therefore questioning God's judgment. He states that "God rebukes our thoughts." The plural pronoun "our" would be representative of himself, or any other Christian. It is important to recognize whom he applies this verse to, for he applies it to Christians who question God's judgment. It becomes apparent that this is Nettleton's "whipping lash" upon any person who would disagree with his philosophy of election to salvation.

In examining Psalm 50, two things become apparent:

a. The fact that Nettleton took one line and quoted it, out of an entire verse.

b. In examining the context, we find that these verses are speaking about the mind and thinking of the lost; *not the saved*, and reveals Nettleton's misuse and disregard of the context.

Now let us examine the context with Verses 16 and 20:

"But unto the wicked God saith, What hast thou to do to declare my statutes, or that thou shouldest take my covenant in thy mouth? (16)"

"Seeing thou hatest instruction, and castest my words behind thee. When thou sawest a thief, then thou consentest with him, and hast been partaker with adulterers. Thou givest thy mouth to evil, and thy tongue frameth deceit. Thou sittest and speakest against thy brother; thou slanderest thine own mother's son." (20)

Now let us go to Verse 21 where Mr. Nettleton extracts only one line and examine the whole verse:

"These things hast thou done, and I kept silence; thou thoughtest that I was altogether such as one as thyself: (They reduced God to humanity.) and set them in order before thine eyes."

172

Notice Verse 22:

"Now consider this, ye that forget God, lest I tear you in pieces, and there be none to deliver."

These verses reveal that God is speaking to the wicked. He, then, reveals what they are thinking concerning Him! Nettleton applies their reasoning toward God as being our reasoning--if we disagree with his doctrine of election. This is unbelievable! In other words, if one disagrees with Mr. Nettleton's, they are one of the wicked because they are thinking just like those in Psalm 50:16-22.

In summary, Mr. Nettleton has taken a piece of Scripture as a mental "whipping lash" with reverse psychology to slap any who dare to disagree with his man-made doctrine of election. I hope you can begin to see how important it is to take Scripture in its context. One can construct any doctrine they wish by quoting little pieces of Scripture, phrases out of verses, to endorse their own philosophy.

In 2 Timothy 2:15 we are reminded to:

"Study to shew thyself approved unto God, a workman that needeth not to be ashamed, rightly dividing the word of truth."

Rightly dividing the Word of God does not mean putting it on the chopping block and grabbing whatever piece I can to support my ideas.

2.   Uncertainty of Scripture

On page 34 of his book, Mr. Nettleton makes a very interesting statement. I quote:

"While it may not be logical to insist that all the verses cited prove the doctrine of election, yet surely the conclusion should be drawn that the doctrine of election is taught in the Bible."

173

This statement seems to me to be kind of con-tradictory. Why would Nettleton use certain Scriptures (in an attempt to support the doctrine of election) after just making the statement:

"While it may not be logical to insist that all the verses cited prove the doctrine of election..."

My question is, "Why, then, did he use these verses, tying them in as weight to endorse his doctrine of election, if they do not necessarily prove that doctrine? As dogmatically as Nettleton writes concerning his position on election, I would think that he would use Scriptures that would be unquestionable, even to his own mind. But such is not the case. It is hard to imagine that one would use Scripture to support a major doctrine and then turn around and say, "I am not sure if all these Scriptures support it or not." Can one imagine the confusion in which the reader is left?

We know that:

"All scripture is given by inspiration of God, and is profitable for doctrine, for reproof , for correction, for instruction in righteousness." - 2 Timothy 3:16

Since all Scripture is given by the inspiration of God, His Word in one place cannot contradict His Word in another place. With the proper interpretation and Bible study, the above statement by Mr. Nettleton would become unnecessary and reveals how unstable his thinking really is.

3. Reading into the Scriptures

In Nettleton's book, on page 161, he quotes Acts 18:9-11 and then gives his assessment of what the verses teach:

"Then spake the Lord to Paul in the night by a vision, be not afraid, but speak, and hold not thy peace: For I am with thee, and no man shall set on thee to hurt thee: for I have much people in this city. And he continued there a year and

174

six months, teaching the Word of God among them." - Acts 18:9-11

Here are Nettleton's words concerning these verses:

"It was predetermined that Paul would have success in Corinth. God assured him that he had much people there. Did this dull the edge of Paul's evangelism? Not at all. The opposite being true. Being assured God had chosen many to salvation, Paul set out to reap the harvest."

The error that Nettleton makes is in saying that, "God had chosen many to salvation." In re-reading these Scriptures, I do not find Nettleton's words in these verses anywhere. In God's foreknowledge, He knows everyone who is going to be saved. But never does God choose those to be saved, over-riding their free will. Notice in Verses 12 and 13:

"And when Gallio was the deputy of Achaia, the Jews made insurrection with one accord against Paul, and brought him to the judgment seat. Saying, this fellow persuadeth men to worship God contrary to the law."

Notice the words *"persuaded men to worship God."* You see, the Jews accused Paul of *persuading men* to worship God. Why would Paul have to persuade men to worship God if they were already elected to do so? Nettleton says God has chosen some to salvation, but the Scriptures he quoted do not say that. God's warning to every Christian of the danger in believing man's ideas, instead of the inerrant Word of God is found in Jeremiah 17:5...

"Thus saith the Lord; Cursed be the man that trusteth in man, and maketh flesh his arm, and whose heart departeth from the Lord." - Jeremiah 17:5

God, in his omniscience, knew that there would be people saved in that city. In Verse 9 the Lord spoke to Paul at night by a vision. Today, the Lord does not speak to us in visions, but speaks to us by His Word. In Isaiah 55:11 we are told:

175

"So shall my word be that goeth forth out of my mouth: it shall not return unto me void, but it shall accomplish that which I please, and it shall prosper in the thing whereto I sent it."

The New Testament instructs us in 2 Timothy 4:2,3:

"Preach the word; be instant in season, out of season; reprove, rebuke, exhort with all longsuffering and doctrine. For the time will come when they will not endure sound doctrine; but after their own lusts shall they heap to themselves teachers, having itching ears."

Our commandment is to *"Preach the word."* People will be saved by hearing the Word of God preached, just as there will be people who reject it. Nevertheless, we are assured by the Word of God that it will not return void. Our command is to tell everyone the good news of Jesus Christ. God's will is revealed in Mark 16:15...

"And he said unto them, go ye into all the world, and preach the gospel to every creature."

Those endorsing election would reason away this verse by saying that we are to witness to every creature since we do not know whom God has chosen to be saved. That kind of reasoning disintegrates in light of God's answer to such foolishness as recorded in 1 Timothy 2:3,4:

"For this is good and acceptable in the sight of God our Saviour: Who will have all men to be saved, and to come unto the knowledge of the truth."

I choose to agree with God's Word and will, that He would have *"all men"* to be saved. What about you? For election to salvation to be true, God would have to go against His own will. Unthinkable!

4. Human Reasoning and Double-Talk

I would like to quote two paragraphs by Mr. Nettleton from page 162 of his book. These reveal the confusion which results from endorsing *Chosen to Salvation:*

"There is a great danger of depending on self, on human wisdom and human ability, but 'salvation is of the Lord' and we must depend upon the reproving (convicting) work of the Spirit of God. Since God has chosen some to be saved, He will carry out His plan. He will, by His Spirit, do a work of grace in hearts. God will do it. We as earthen vessels will give him the glory. Dependence on God makes man dependent on prayer. We appropriate power and wisdom from heaven for our task. It is still wise to plead with God for souls."

Keep in mind that what we have just quoted are Nettleton's words, not God's. Since, Nettleton says, God has chosen some to be saved and He will carry out His plan; then, turn around and tell me it is wise to plead with God for souls-- may I ask, "WHY?" Since God's mind is supposedly already made up, why would it do any good to plead with God for someone else to be saved? Would I be pleading with God to change His mind? If so, then the doctrine of election would not be true. Therefore, God's election before the foundation of the world could be changed by my pleading at this present time. To put it bluntly, this is just plain, old-fashioned double-talk which only leads a Christian into the arena of confusion! Can you see how this doctrine crumbles under the Light of the Word of God.

On one hand, if God has elected certain ones to be saved and that cannot be altered--why would Nettleton tell me that it is always wise to plead for souls? This would be ridiculous! On the other hand, if God's election can be altered, then it evidently depends on the free will of man to choose or

177

reject Christ. Either way you go, the doctrine of election for salvation is excluded and the free will of man is illuminated.

5. An Un-Wise Evangelist

May I quote Mr. Nettleton's words on page 162 on his book:

> "A wise evangelist once said, 'I believe more in pleading with God for men than I do in pleading with men for God.' One does not exclude the other. We must still plead with men."

The quote from a "wise evangelist" is, first all, not Biblical. It is just another "cute cliché." A line of double-talk which is illogical because it has no Biblical foundation whatsoever. In fact, it is contrary to the Word of God. Notice in Luke 14:23...

> *"And the lord said unto the servant, go out into the highways and hedges, and <u>compel</u> <u>them</u> <u>to</u> <u>come</u> <u>in</u>, that my house may be filled."*

We now have a free will to make a decision as to who is wise; the evangelist or the Lord in Luke 14:23. Whoever this evangelist was, he must never have read the book of Acts. For in doing so, one would find the Apostle Paul continually reasoning with the Jews in the synagogues and pleading with men wherever he went to put their trust in Christ. This so-called "wise evangelist" would be wise to reverse his statement and align his thinking with God's Word. There is nothing complicated or mysterious about the Word of God or the will of God. The false "doctrine of election to salvation" is contrary to both.

There is nothing complicated about the foreknowledge and omniscience of God. He knows the end from beginning. He knows everything about everything. He knows who is going to be saved and who is not going to be saved. However, He *never* infringes His foreknowledge upon the free will of man, as foreknowledge is not predestination.

Can one reconcile the sovereignty of God and the free will of man? Absolutely! As long as one does not take the sovereignty of God and make God contradict Himself. Can God contradict Himself? The answer--"No, He cannot!" For example, we are told in Genesis 9:15...

> *"And I will remember my covenant, which is between me and you and every living creature of all flesh; and the waters shall no more become a flood to destroy all flesh."*

You see, God can never destroy the earth by water again. There are many things God cannot do because He has limited Himself by stating that He would not do them. God does not come back, years later, and contradict Himself. If God elected some to be saved, He definitely would have contradicted Himself when He tells us in 2 Peter 3:9 that He is

> *"...not willing that any should perish, but that all should come to repentance."*

Some try to reconcile the sovereignty of God and the free will of man by taking the "middle road." This is what Nettleton does. He does not deny that we are to take the Gospel to every creature, but attempts to go right down the middle of the road, "straddling the fence," in an attempt to reconcile the doctrine of election with the free will of man. Nettleton asserts that what we cannot understand about God's election:

> "We must take it by faith" (page 14).

If we do not, then we are bringing God down to our level. As Nettleton states on page 14:

> "We are prone to pattern God after ourselves. We create God in our image and likeness."

This is his philosophy. Then we are slapped in the face with the accusation that God is not pleased with us for doing that--or as he states: "God rebukes our thoughts." One <u>must</u> remember that these are Nettleton's words, not God's.

In short, Nettleton mixes bits and pieces of Scripture with a cup of philosophy as his foundation for "election to salvation." The Word of God disintegrates between man-made doctrine built upon the sands of human wisdom instead of His Word.

> *"For it is written, I will destroy the wisdom of the wise, and will bring to nothing the understanding of the prudent."*
> *1 Corinthians 1:19*

6.   Nettleton's Psychology

A bit of philosophy by Dr. Nettleton is also found on page 142 of his book. I would like to quote two paragraphs for analyzation:

> "Some will reason that if God did not elect all, He did not love all. One might as well reason that if God doesn't save all, God doesn't love all. Our system of doctrine should not depend on that which some men call steps of logic, but on clear statements of the Bible which supersede human reasoning."

The only trouble with this reasoning is, the logic that Nettleton uses is really logic against himself. When he says that, "Some will reason that if God did not elect all, He did not love all," that is entirely true. This is good reasoning. When you believe that God elected some to be saved and not others, it is the most logical thing in the world that God did not love the others. Remember, this logical conclusion is in reference to a false doctrine.

Nettleton attempts to discredit any logical conclusion that would discredit his endorsement of election. If God elected to save some and not others, then it logically can be concluded that "If God doesn't save all, God doesn't love all." Nettleton says this kind of logic is faulty because it is based on human reasoning. The problem lies not in faulty logic; but, rather, in the faulty doctrine of election projected by Nettleton.

Carrying Nettleton's philosophy to a conclusion--it would not be logical to believe God's Word because it refutes his doctrine of "election to salvation." God's simple Word incorporates excellent reasoning and good logic. For "His love for all" is proven by His "invitation to all" to be saved. Notice in John 3:16,17:

> "For _God_ _so_ _loved_ _the_ _world_, that he gave his only begotten Son, that _whosoever_ believeth in him should not perish, but have everlasting life. (16) For God sent not His Son into the world to condemn the world; but that _the_ _world_ _through_ _him_ _might_ _be_ _saved_." (17)

Someone has rightly said, "When common sense makes good sense, seek no other sense." These two verses reveal to us that God loves everyone in the world, and His desire is that everyone might be saved. He also informs us that whosoever believeth in Him should not perish, but have everlasting life. It is God's will that everyone be saved, but it is their free will to except or reject Him. These clear statements reveal God's love, purpose and will do not supersede human reasoning and are in perfect accordance with rational reasoning and logic.

7. No Peace If You Disagree With Nettleton

Mr. Nettleton states that there can be no peace of mind to those who resist his position of election, therefore, resisting the Word of God. Here are his words from page 160 of his book:

> "Yet the word of God mentions it (being chosen to salvation) many times, and there can be no peace of mind when the word of God is resisted."

In reiterating his position he further states:

"God reminds us that He was at work behind the scenes, planning it all before the world began: 'As many as were ordained to eternal life believed' (Acts 13:48). That settles it."

(For our coverage of Acts 13:48, see pages 63 and 64). I am then assured by Nettleton that I can have peace if I submit and believe as he does. His words on page 160:

"When the struggle is over, even though the mind can by no means grasp it all, there is peace in believing."

Here, again, his accusations are asserted and not God's Word. I would like to know how Nettleton obtained the omniscience to know the mind and accuse those who oppose his position of being void of this so-called peace! In other words, the great Bible teachers, preachers and Christians who oppose "Chosen to Salvation" will never experience the peace of those who endorse it. For one to make an accusation such as this is, to say the very least, unbelievable! I hardly think I would have taken the time to answer Mr. Nettleton's book if I did not have a peace in doing so.

One could incorporate Nettleton's philosophy and use it in reverse, i.e., we hope he will see his error in election and then he can experience the peace we enjoy!

Here is where many saints falter in their witnessing. They read something or other in the Word about predestination and then they reason that God predestinates some people to be saved, and thus predestinates some people to be lost. This is not the case. To begin with, predestination is never for the lost man; but rather, predestination is for the saved men. We have only to read our Bibles, and read the context where it is speaking of predestination, to clearly understand that Salvation is, indeed, a personal matter based upon the "whosoever wills."

- Dr. Mark G. Cambron

"False Doctrine Shipwrecks Souls"

"For so hath the Lord commanded us, saying, I have set thee to be a light of the Gentiles, that thou shouldest be for salvation unto the ends of the earth." - Acts 13:47

"False Doctrine Shipwrecks Souls"

CHAPTER SIX

SUMMARY

As you have read through this book, I am sure you have noticed the repetition of some verses. This was done, purposely, for emphasis. verses that reveal God's will and man's free will should be gone over and memorized for ready use in opposition to this false doctrine. The more Scriptures you are familiar with, the more difficult it will be for Nettleton and others to extract bits and pieces of Scripture on which to build their false doctrine of election.

The "doctrine of election to salvation" places Scripture in one place in direct opposition with Scripture in other places. For example, in 2 Peter 3:9 the Lord said He is...

> "...<u>not</u> <u>willing</u> that <u>any</u> <u>should</u> <u>perish</u>, but that all should come to repentance (i.e., a change of mind)."

If it is not God's will that any should perish, then why did He fail to elect the ones who <u>are</u> going to perish? The election people will throw the contradiction <u>they</u> have created back on God so He can take full responsibility for the false doctrine <u>they</u> have manufactured. They tell us it is a deep doctrine, as we cannot understand God's mind! Nettleton's words on page 165 would seem to verify this:

"When we consider the doctrine of election, we are studying the deepest doctrinal matter of time and eternity. The very nature of God is facing us, and His ways 'past finding out."

Nettleton would have you believe that you cannot understand God's ways, yet God disagrees with Nettleton by _revealing_ to us His ways. God has revealed that all mankind has sinned (Romans 3:23). God has revealed that the wages of sin is death (Romans 6:23). God has revealed that He loves the world (all sinners). God has revealed that Christ paid for the sins of the _world_. God has revealed that anyone (whosoever) may have eternal life (John 3:16). In conclusion, Nettleton's philosophy fades away as God's will surfaces and illuminates...

"Who will have all men to saved, and to come unto the knowledge of the truth." – 1 Timothy 2:4

Misuse of Scripture Comes Home to Haunt the Guilty!

Almost every book I have read endorsing election for salvation uses Romans, Chapter 9. Two verses almost universally quoted, in part or et al, are:

"...Jacob have I loved, but Esau have I hated." -Romans 9:13

"Therefore hath he mercy on whom he will have mercy, and whom he will he hardeneth." - Romans 9:18

Bear with me, briefly, as we will return to these two verses shortly. Nettleton reveals that there is a division within the election camp. On page 20 of his book he states some endorsing election believe in a limited atonement; while he, himself, and the majority do not. In other words, they propose that Christ died for all; but chose only some to be saved. Most admit that Christ died for all because He loved all (the world). The same people who say this use Romans 9:13 and 18 to endorse their doctrine of election and contradict themselves.

Sometimes these people strain a gnat and swallow a camel! When election people say that God loves all and then grab Romans 9:13 that states *"Esau have I hated,"* something is wrong. Remember, those endorsing election use this to support their doctrine. If God loves the world, how can it be reconciled that he hated Esau? How mixed up can one get? The verse they use (along with Verse 18) to support their doctrine actually refutes their false doctrine (For our coverage of Romans 9, see pages 75-87).

Two possibilities:

God became confused. He loved the world, but forgot about Esau, whom He hated. Impossible! Esau was included in God's loving the world.

Election advocates have obviously misused Romans 9:13 and 18, as it cannot be speaking of salvation or God contradicted Himself. All false doctrine is built upon misapplication of Scripture, extracted out of context. In their eagerness to support election they have misused Scripture which, in turn, has returned to haunt the guilty!

Whenever you read a book and you notice the author extracting bits and pieces of Scripture, continuously-- beware! Stop immediately--go to the Bible and start examining the context. The above is only one simple illustration.

Beware! In his book *Chosen to Salvation*, Nettleton wastes no words in attacking those who oppose his position on election. In other words, those who would dare to speak out against him would be guilty of sin. Nettleton's words on page 15 are piercing!...

"Is it not a sin to cry out against a man who promotes the Bible doctrine of election?

One the next page (157), the last line of Nettleton's book, he states:

"God grants us wisdom. God gives us love and understanding."

On one page, anyone who disagrees with Nettleton has committed sin. On the very next page he is asking for wisdom, love and understanding. Maybe if he had asked for wisdom, love and understanding first, the rest of us who oppose his position could have escaped his verdict: guilty of sin!

Nettleton's Doctrine of Election Promoted

On the back of Nettleton's book appears the following:

"Dr. Nettleton's writings include Sunday School Curriculum for Regular Baptist Press, and articles for the Baptist Bulletin."

After writing an entire book endorsing election, you can rest assured, Nettleton's teachings will surface in his Sunday School material. You have a choice to make--do you want your children taught the doctrine of election for salvation in Sunday School? Allow me to challenge you to recapitulate over your Sunday School material to see how much of Nettleton's teaching you can discover. You, then, have a choice--will you stand on your convictions equally as strong as Nettleton does? May we always be comforted by God's Word when speaking out against false doctrine.

"So that we may boldly say, The Lord is my helper, and I will not fear what man shall do unto me." - Hebrews 13:6

We are now faced with a decision:

"For do I now persuade men, or God? or do I seek to please men? for if I yet pleased men, I should not be the servant of Christ."

How sad when we talk about our teenagers and the peer pressure they face; but bow ourselves to the peer pressure of organizations and fellowships. God gave us a free will and we are held fully responsible for the decisions we make (Psalms 118:8 and Proverbs 30:6).

"It is better to trust in the Lord than to put confidence in man." - Psalm 118:8

"Add thou not unto his words, lest he reprove thee, and thou be found a liar." - Proverbs 30:6

"False Doctrine Shipwrecks Souls"

A WISE EVANGELIST

As stated before, Predestination is for the saved man. God knows who is going to be saved, and thus He has predestined certain blessings for those who are going to get saved by faith. In other words, God draws a circle, figuratively speaking, and says that whosoever believes in the Lord Jesus Christ will get in the circle. So the believer, upon his faith in Jesus Christ, steps into the circle. Then God says, figuratively speaking, "Whosoever is in that circle by faith, I have predestinated that they shall receive these blessings," and here they are:

- Dr. Mark G. Cambron

"False Doctrine Shipwrecks Souls"

SCRIPTURE INDEX

191

SCRIPTURE INDEX

SCRIPTURE INDEX

SCRIPTURE INDEX

SCRIPTURE INDEX

BIBLIOGRAPHY

1. *Chosen to Salvation, Select Thoughts on the Doctrine of Election,* by David Nettleton, Regular Baptist Press, Schaumburg, IL 1983

2. Poem, *The Lighthouse of God's Word,* by Marjorie A. Younce, 2010

3. *The Bible, the King James Translation.* God's Word is more than sufficient to expound the truth and expose those who would pervert the truth.

4. *An Expository Dictionary of New Testament Words, with their Precise Meanings for English Readers,* by W.E. Vine, M.A., Fleming H. Revell Company

5. *Foreknowledge, Predestination, and Election,* Article by Dr. Mark G. Cambron, selected quotes.

6. *Personal Evangelism Handbook,* by Dr. A. Ray Stanford, selected quotes.

7. *Strong's Exhaustive Concordance*